SPEAKING OUT!

"What you all did by walking away was to tell us our situation wasn't real, and there's only one possible reason for that. It's because we're gay. You ignored the real feelings we were working out as people, because you decided that gay people's problems with each other weren't your concern. Well, you're wrong.

"Problems are problems, and people are people, and what happened between Ralph and me could have taught you all something but you blew it, all of you.

"You blew it because you're prejudiced. You think our lives are just imitations of yours and that our feelings aren't real. Well, I'm telling you they are. I'm standing right here in front of you, and I'm a real human being, and I'm a real homosexual. . . ."

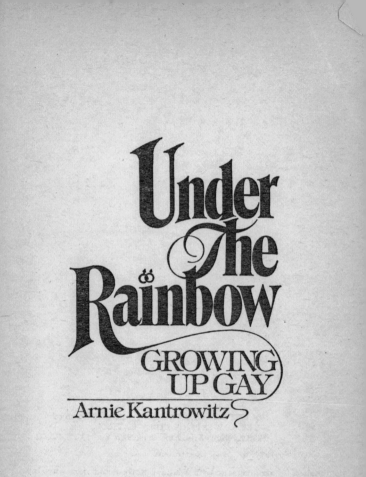

Under The Rainbow

GROWING UP GAY

Arnie Kantrowitz

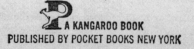

A KANGAROO BOOK
PUBLISHED BY POCKET BOOKS NEW YORK

Partial support for this project was provided
by a grant from the State University of New
York Research Foundation Joint Awards Council.

Copyright © 1977 by Arnie Kantrowitz

Published by arrangement with William Morrow and Company, Inc.
Library of Congress Catalog Card Number: 76-30442

ISBN: 0-671-81965-8

First Pocket Books printing July, 1978

Trademarks registered in the United States and other countries.

Printed in the U.S.A.

For Jim and Vito,
and
For Everyone in These Pages
with Love

"Somewhere over the rainbow, skies are blue,
and the dreams that you dare to dream
really do come true.

Somewhere over the rainbow, bluebirds fly.
Birds fly over the rainbow:
why, then, oh why can't I?"

—E. Y. HARBURG / HAROLD ARLEN*

I have changed the names of some people and of the places where they live in order to protect their privacy. But the actual facts of my life were recorded here as faithfully as memory made possible.

A. K.

1

AT FIRST GLANCE CHRISTOPHER STREET LOOKS ONLY slightly out of the ordinary, like any other Greenwich Village street. But it's someplace very special. Once, seduced by its magic, I could have sworn that it was an enchanted road to paradise, paved with yellow brick. Now, from the windows of my apartment overlooking it, I can see it for what it is: the most honest street I have ever walked. On a good night a thousand men come here to parade their secret lives in public. They dress as their erotic fantasies: as cowboys, freaks, or motorcyclists, as women, or just as themselves. If they are lucky, two of them will meet each other and go home for some sex. If I'm lucky, I am one of them. When I go out cruising, I like to imagine I look something like a lumberjack with the sleeves of my flannel shirt rolled up; but I'm an English teacher, "a nice Jewish boy." I don't know why my life turned out so much more exciting to live than the one I was raised for. Fate, maybe. All I know is that when I walk to the pier at the end of Christopher Street and look across the Hudson to the drab industrial skyline of

New Jersey, where I was born, I invariably shudder as I remember one of my friends quipping, "How'd you like to click your ruby heels together and wind up back in Newark?"

My family was a Freudian classic. Both my parents were difficult to love. My father was withdrawn and uncommunicative; my mother filled the household with fishwife accusations of failure. He wasn't too good at business; she measured men according to their success. Success was the most important thing in my mother's life. It was always on the other side of the rainbow, where mortals can't reach, but that didn't stop her.

Hannah Brockoff's version of the American Dream was nurtured by necessity. She was born in the Soviet Union, in a town called Chartria, the youngest of six sisters and two brothers. Her oldest brother came to America first and then sent for my grandparents, who left their seven other children, including my mother, who was still a baby, to fend for themselves until they could be sent for. My mother was seven years old before she saw her mother again. I must have heard the story a thousand times about how she had to borrow a pair of socks from the richest girl in town and improvise a pair of cardboard shoes so she could pose properly for the passport photo.

They called America the *Goldene Medina,* the land whose streets were paved with gold. They landed in Newark. Instead of gold, they found a depression. My grandfather tried to run a candy store but was too busy addressing God to provide much more than potatoes for supper, and my grandmother stalwartly plucked chicken feathers at the neighborhood butcher shop.

Even from her own descriptions my mother was an incipient Emma Bovary as a child. She resented the one hand-me-down dress that she washed every night for school. She wanted the piano her classmate owned. She envied the mothers who spoke English and the sisters without accents whom her friends could bring to school with pride, and she dreaded the epithet "greenhorn." She hid in the cloakroom, ashamed of her lunch of black bread and chicken fat. Her dreams were forged in twenty-five-cent movie matinees that offered fantasies of everything that was missing in her own life. There could never be enough clothes in the closet, enough silver in the breakfront, enough Fleetwood in the garage to make up for her poverty.

By the time she was sixteen the name had become Ann, and she was able to buy a clock, a curtain, and a counter, rent a store, and open a dry-cleaning shop. Simon Kantrowitz, a real estate broker with an office, came in one day in 1939, soon introduced her to his son Sydney, who boasted the promise of becoming a lawyer, and, with visions of middle-class matronhood sparkling in her naïve eyes, they were married before the year was out. Her mother was too busy to come to the wedding.

My father failed the bar and never became a lawyer. Instead he drove a laundry truck.

The morning after the wedding night, my mother told me, she woke in their top-floor apartment on Clinton Place to find my father gone. He was downstairs visiting his mother. That episode began a battle of many years for my father's allegiance, which lasted until Grandma Sarah's death. I had to put salt in my pocket whenever I went to Grandma's house, to ward off the Evil Eye. My mother attacked her mother-in-law for using guilt, in the form of "Look how much I've done for you but I'm not complaining. What's a mother for?" Then she told me it hadn't been much fun for her to wheel a baby carriage, recovering from the seventeen hours of unanesthetized labor it took to deliver me, while her teen-aged friends were jitterbug-

ging at the malt-shop jukebox. But she wasn't complaining. What's a mother for?

My father could never meet her craving for material
security. All he cared about, she accused, was enough
to eat and a place to sleep. But then he didn't have her
motivation. He was fourteen years older than she and
was raised during the boom of the Roaring Twenties.
Grandpa Simon had begun as a carpenter and had
made himself into a real estate entrepreneur, and they
had had the first car in the neighborhood. By the time
he had lost his money, in the crash of '29, his children
were too old to believe in the desperation of poverty
and lived in the eternal temporary setback of genteel
want.

I don't know if my father met my mother's craving
for romance, but she had probably forsaken that for
more practical priorities anyway. She was beautiful to
me then, her long dark-blond hair done in a pageboy,
artful arches above her big Bette Davis green eyes, a
prominent Semitic nose fitting well above her Lana
Turner lips, painted in dark 1940's lipstick. The square-
shouldered, V-necked dresses were covered with rose-
buds and femininity. My father was two inches shorter
than she and squarely built. His body boasted a heavy
coat of hair, and he smoked cigars. He saw the world
through cool blue eyes set above his plain, even features, eyes that might twinkle, but which did so only
when he clowned in time-honored Yiddish fashion for
his family on the bottom floor of the house on Clinton
Place. "Jewish" would have been no more than a label,
but I was a child in World War II, born at the end of
1940, growing to awareness just at the time when the
horrors of the Nazi concentration camps were whispered in uncertain tones, a time when it was puzzling
to be both Jewish and alive.

My father worked in a munitions plant during the

war and then took to the road to work for the state
fairs with a game that consisted of trying to cover a red
circle painted on a white board by dropping slate disks
onto it. I never saw anyone do it successfully. My father's secret was probably quick hands and lots of dou-
bletalk. Mostly, though, he wasn't around. He would
come back from his trips with a gift of a few comic
books for me, and I was always too embarrassed to
tell him I had already read them.

Often my mother took me to the movies. On the
way she might point out a white-haired old couple
helping each other along the sidewalk. She always
noticed old people. Her eyes would mist instantly and
she would sigh, "After a long life together, to still love
each other like that. . . ." She was in love with love.
She saw herself as the suffering heroine in a love story,
and exposure to her fantasies taught me to do the same.
I developed that strange, wish-frosted vision of love
that novels of the nineteenth century had taught. My
mother inherited most of them via Hollywood's versions, or more vulgarly from magazines like *True Romances,* which, with mildly lurid suggestion, taught her
everything her marriage failed to be. Later she would
abandon her pulp stories along with her pageboy, but
she would never lose her secret belief that she had been
cheated of her proper portion. She felt like a maiden
in a tower, which is a far cry from the housewife in the
third-floor walk-up.

We had moved to the third story of a modest two-
and-a-half-family house on the southernmost block of
Newark. Our living room was unpretentious, decorated
with blue-mirrored tabletops and a velveteen couch with
palm-tree slipcovers. But my mother had taken us both
to the movies. Deep in our hearts lurked the image of
a vine-covered cottage, picket-fenced garden, gingham
apron and all. It might be in Munchkinland modern,

but that didn't matter. It had kitchens where grease never spattered from the frying pans and dishes never broke; and it had bedrooms where you could lovingly remember last night's embraces while you tightened up the sheets. And of course it had *him*. Always about to come home. (We lived in eternal anticipation, never in plain reality.) His features would be more perfect than yesterday, his love more true. The final embrace would be perfect; and that's how it would stay forever when the gold brocade curtains swept closed across the screen and the houselights came up: frozen, under THE END.

Of course there was a minor hitch in my adopting those fantasies. I was a boy.

But what would I have given to be Merle Oberon, dying perfectly in Olivier's arms, in rerun after rerun? What wouldn't my mother have given? She wanted to be Scarlett O'Hara, carried up her ostentatious stairs. Those fantasies sustained us both through years when real emotions seemed lean. The escape into fiction and film provided an exercise for an imagination that was starving, because lodged in its throat was the notion that life should imitate art, and nothing of substance could pass, only perfection.

During my childhood I spent Saturday afternoons at the Mayfair Theater and the Park Theater, as we moved to different parts of Newark. I learned my multiplication tables and where the Nile River is from the texts of Maple Avenue School, but I learned my feelings at the movies. And I learned my feelings well, in Technicolor with music and costumes and handsome leading men, with their trim moustaches and their devilish bedroom eyes, with their wind-blown hair and the aura of genius about them. I wanted Rhett Butler to sweep me away from Atlanta ablaze; I wanted Heathcliff sobbing on my grave.

My fantasies . . . how dear they were to me! . . . were like old friends. They began to rule my life secretly from within. And all of it started at the movies—the Saturday matinees—and at the children's room in the library. The fairy tales, the dog stories, the comics, the serials, Tarzan, Flash Gordon, Clark Gable. They were all one piece. My mind swallowed them whole. I was more than merely alive, because my images were larger than life, their heroism magnified into giant models on the screen. The women in swirling gowns I wanted to swirl in; the men I wanted as my lovers, as myself matured.

Imagining myself the pirate's captive in the ship whose sails billow against a Technicolor blue sky . . . knowing my hair was not Rita Hayworth's, but imagining it was, and my dimple—if only I had one, he would . . . my dimple Lana Turner's and my Ava Gardner knowing eyes. I thought I wasn't beautiful enough; I was fat. He would never hold me; I would never look like her. Like my mommy, like a lady in the movies, with lipstick, who smells so pretty. (My daddy is away.) And this upturned table is a ship, and all my favorite things are on it, and I'm safe, and the blue, blue linoleum is a sea, and he is sailing toward me in a pirate ship, and he owns me. I am his, but I want him to want me, my pirate hero, my father. I would do anything. I tried to suffer. I suffered like Ida Lupino suffered. I suffered like Claire Trevor suffered. Like Barbara Stanwyck. I coped like Susan Hayward. I ached like Judy Garland. I endured like Bette Davis. And it only took a little translating to make it gay. It only took defying everything I'd ever been told.

That wasn't me daydreaming in the folding cot with the metal frame and the yellow chenille bedspread, trimmed with the sporadic fringe that had survived the wash. It was Margaret O'Brien in ribbons and pinafore,

...he window seat of an English country manor ...and down the walk is a secret garden, and the ...s so snug and secure, the lawn so forever neat and ...en, and . . . your mother wants you to play baseball.

We lived on Grumman Avenue, a placid, pleasant neighborhood, full of children to play with. I liked jump rope. They bought me a cowboy outfit. The cap pistol was okay, but the arguments over whether you got me and I'm dead were boring. I much preferred playing house with the girls in the garage, even if they always made me the daddy. Tending to a family seemed so much nicer than scorekeeping the dead. But it wasn't all right to play house. Little boys aren't supposed to. Almost every night when I came home for supper, I was interrogated about whom I had played with, what I had played, and for how long. It was easier to lie, so I could do what I wanted to do, but my inquisitor didn't believe me. Her cardinal rule was, "Just tell the truth, and you won't be punished." Now I live by it.

She bought me a baseball uniform and led me up to the other end of the street where the big boys played. Begging their indulgence, she planted me in the middle of their game. I didn't know them. I didn't know the game. No one had taught me. I cried. I didn't much like baseball anyway, and I liked uniforms even less.

I escaped more deeply into my own fantasies. I passed through the usual stage of deciding I had been adopted by strangers and took it one step further. I imagined I was really the child of the King and Queen of Earth, the heir apparent, and that I was being raised in humble circumstances to temper my understanding of my future subjects so that I would be a wise and compassionate ruler. I fantasized that anyone I encountered during the day was actually someone being rewarded for heroism—the more involved they were with my life, the greater their deed, with rewards rang-ing from being seen on the street, to eye contact, to an exchange of words, or even feelings. I had been taken to the movies.

During the war years I was tucked into nursery schools, boarding farms, and day camps, but none of them worked. I always had to leave as soon as I arrived because I wanted to be near my mother. She was so beautiful. When the Zenith radio announced that Franklin Delano Roosevelt was dead, I remember she cried. (My mother went in for presidents in a big bipartisan way.) I wanted to join her out of sympathy, but I had been training myself not to cry. It wasn't manly to show emotions, not even for the European holocaust which was mercifully rendered unreal by its distance. Europe was where children starved if I didn't finish my cereal. When the war ended, I was five years old.

I was six years old the first time I seduced a man. I even remember his name: it was Larry. He was fourteen and lived up the street from me, and he was beautiful. He made me feel coy and flirtatious, which came out as hero worship and tagging along, the only means available for expressing your lust when you're six. One summer day after watching him play ball, I walked home with him, hinting broadly that I would like him to take me down to his cellar.

"What for?" he wanted to know.

"Just to play," said I.

"Play what?" he persisted.

"Oh, whatever we think of," I said as suggestively as I could, though I scarcely knew what I was suggesting. I only knew I wanted him to protect and overpower me.

"Well . . ." he conceded. "Supper isn't for a while. Okay."

He was the pirate captain, and I was captured from another vessel, and inside the coal room, when I was caught, I managed to feel his embrace as he tied me up and "tortured" me by holding a lighted match far enough away so it could do no harm. Not quite Paulette Goddard, but respectable for openers.

The first time a man tried to seduce me was not long afterward. I was walking in my short shorts past the school playground near Grandpa Simon's house when I passed the proverbial black sedan parked menacingly near the curb. The driver beckoned to me.

"Want to go for a ride?" he invited suggestively.

"My mother told me not to ride with strangers," I answered, obedient to the most stringent caution I had been taught.

"I've got what you want," he leered.

I was totally naïve. "What do I want?"

"You know. . . ."

"No, I don't," I said, walking off firmly.

It was about that time that my mother first tried to counsel me about the evils of making love to someone of your own sex. The message wasn't specific, and I wouldn't have understood it if it were, but it was clear. My guts understood it all too well.

"Arnold," she began with import, "you know there are certain ways little boys are supposed to behave. You know what little boys who don't behave right are called? They're called sissies."

I didn't know what she was talking about, yet I knew exactly what she meant. I was different from what she wanted me to be, and I was scared, scared there was something wrong with me, scared my mother didn't love me.

"When I was in high school," she continued, "there was a boy named Arthur, and Arthur didn't act the way he was supposed to. All the other kids called him a sissy and laughed at him. And one day a gang of them followed him home from school, and somebody threw a rock at him, and it hit him in the head and killed him. You don't want that to happen to you, do you?"

"No, Mommy."

"Then you'll behave the way you're supposed to, won't you?"

"Yes, Mommy."

I have never buried the story of Arthur very deep in my memory. It always lingers just near the surface, and I am reminded of it often, when I hear children call each other "sissy" or adults call each other "faggot." What an act of defiance it takes actually to be those things and assert them, and how strengthening that is! Yes, Mommy, I'll behave the way I'm supposed to: the way *I'm* supposed to.

She finally got the piano she had wanted as a girl—a baby grand—only she had to stand over me with a bread knife to make me practice. My first piano teacher was a tyrant who yelled at me with suffocating garlic breath and rapped my knuckles until I was afraid to play altogether. I traded him in for a kindly old lady who draped Spanish shawls across her piano and spoke softly. I could outfox her easily into letting me practice less, but when it came time to perform at a recital, I was so ill-prepared that I couldn't finish a piece. My mother turned red with angry embarrassment and stopped paying for lessons. Eventually I grew interested on my own, but by then, whenever I sat down at the piano bench, she developed a migraine headache.

When I was seven, I was whisked mysteriously off to my aunt's house. Three days later I was returned home to find my mother in a floor-length pale blue robe dotted with tiny flowers, looking like a movie star at brunch, and in her arms there was a baby. It was news to me.

"Well, now you have just what you've wanted," she said, beaming, "a baby brother. His name is Ira."

Right then and there we began our sibling rivalry. Seven years was too long a span to make playmates of us, but just enough to allow us to compete for her approval in our different arenas. He was the wild one, yelled at but yielded to. I was the impractical one, the wise confidant. But she is contained in each of us. Ira's house looks more like hers than mine does; he shares her goals. But my dreams are more like hers than my brother's are.

Soon after Ira was born, we moved to a two-family house on Mapes Avenue. My father's purchase rescued it from being condemned. The other family in the house also had two sons, Sonny, who was my age, and Paul, who was older. I think it all started when my brother shook his crib around the bedroom and they responded to the noise with a pole banged on their ceiling, but a family feud developed, which escalated until they sliced our laundry up with razor blades. After several years of such skirmishing, they finally moved. Next door. Every time I showed my face at the window at the wrong time, one of them would be there. If I showed my face outside the door at the wrong time, I got beaten up.

My parents were away often, so I was left to my own devices. I went to the movies, looking carefully both ways before I opened my front door. If Sonny and Paul were sitting on their stoop, I sneaked the long way around the block to visit my friend Gerry and tell his parents—who seemed nothing like my own—all the woes of my young life. The rest of the time I stayed home and read. Sonny and Paul were older friends of everyone in the neighborhood, so they were able to organize an army out of the kids on the block to attack our apartment door one terrifying afternoon, while I cowered under the bed, waiting for my parents to return. My mother rescued me.

My father generally stayed at his new grocery store from six-thirty in the morning until ten-thirty at night. To supplement the store's small income, my mother began to take part-time jobs, so I became the baby-sitter for Ira, who was just old enough to demand all my attention. Watching him was nothing like playing house.

I guess it wasn't "house" for my mother either. I guess she didn't like the blue vinyl Hollywood headboards on the twin beds in my room any more than I did, or the old blue-mirrored tables in the living room, re-covered in Leatherette. I know she didn't like the wall I covered with magazine pictures of pretty ladies from the movies, but I wouldn't let her take them down. They were all the beauty I had outside the library and the theater. She did the best she could to make the limitations of reality reach her dreams. She brought a few dollars to an antique shop every week for months to buy a fragile bisque statue of a Napoleonic maiden writing a love letter, with Cupid dictating sweet nothings into her ear from beside her on a flower-covered wall. She had it made into a lamp with an extravagant pink shade. Two boys from the younger set in the neighborhood came to play with my brother. They got into a roughhouse and knocked over the lamp. That's the way with dreams. The baby-sitter got the guilt.

Sometimes my brother took a nap and left me free to indulge my curiosity and investigate the premises. Hidden in the back of my parents' bedroom closet, I found a small booklet with pictures of naked men and ladies doing funny things to each other. It was unusual enough to tuck in my back pocket and take to school. In art class a crowd gathered around the latest oracle, a "Magic Eight Ball" that answered questions with "Yes," "No," or "Maybe" on little tags that floated to the surface of a murky liquid. When the teacher dispersed the crowd, I patted my secret little book to make sure it was safely in my pocket, and she, seeing me, assumed that that was what had been the center of everyone's attention. So the funny little book was confiscated, and I was condemned to days of detention in the principal's office, sitting before his stern puritanical gaze like Hester Prynne in the pillory. The only thing I was guilty of was too much innocence.

At about that time my innocence received yet another blow. We had had a long series of maids, black women of various persuasions and talents. The current one was named Mary, and she was a follower of Father Divine, whose cult proscribed any sexual contact and promised immortality as a reward for abstinence. It was my Edenic custom to wander from bedroom to bathroom naked, utterly unaware of the sinful consequences of exposing my prepubescent body to the light. Mary bore it with grudging silence until she could take it no more and then, in front of my mother, announced to me, "You're a disgrace. I'm gon' thank Father on you if you don' cover your body right up." I didn't know what Father's powers were, but I knew I didn't want him thanked on me. I got dressed. It took another two decades to unlearn that sense of shame. I slept with underwear under my pajamas for years.

That was the time, my mother decided, to tell me the facts of life. My father wasn't about to get into any such raunchy discussion. Mother sat me in the living room with a momentous air and penciled a picture on a wrinkled brown-paper bag, first smoothing it with her long-fingernailed hands. It was a woman's body, or a none-too-erotic facsimile thereof, and in her belly there was a circle with a baby in it.

"Do you know what this is, Arnold?" she asked rhetorically.

"It's a lady."

"That's right. And this lady is going to have a baby . . . just like I had you and your brother."

"But how did the baby get in her belly?" I wanted to know.

"A seed passes between the father and the mother, and the baby grows from the seed." A lot more plausible than storks or cabbages, but not exactly detailed.

"Where does the seed come from?"

"The man makes a white pee-pee." She looked a little exasperated and very embarrassed, but still undaunted.

"Oh. I made a white pee-pee," I said, thinking of a time when my urine had been paler than usual. I was about nine, and she looked at me suspiciously.

"Are you sure?" she inquired.

"Yes. In school, in the boys' room. But it wasn't *very* white." She looked relieved, and she continued patiently with the rest of her lecture.

"I want you to go to the library and get this book," she said, writing *"The Facts of Life and Love for Teenagers* by Evelyn Millis Duvall" on a scrap of the paper bag. "It will explain everything to you." It explained the "Miracle of Birth" with internal diagrams and no lust. It did not explain the miracle of two men loving each other.

But that was the innocent 1940's. My mother came of age in the Fifties. The sweet-young-thing image gave way to the tough-as-nails businesswoman. The rosebud dresses gave way to man-tailored suits with their pencil-slim skirts and their asexually loose single-button jackets. Business was a man's world then. In it, one needed to look at least vaguely like a man. But underneath the loose jacket were the same restraining bras and girdles, and above it the same cosmetic artifice that many women have since learned to minimize in favor of honesty.

Her hair was cut short and set into waves which were combed fleetly back and bleached a blaring blond. In later years it grew again into beehives and bouffants and French twists, but the blond artifice remained for good. She had gone to school to become a real estate "salesman," and eventually she became a broker and opened her own office. There was a lot of wheeling and dealing, and apartment houses came and went, but the primary rewards were a Cadillac and a mink coat, her symbols of success. Like black people who bleached their skin and straightened their hair, she was a Jew of the generation who bleached their hair and straightened their noses. She didn't want to be a "greenhorn." She never had the nose job, much as she wanted it, and she never got my father to shorten the family name, much as she wanted that as well. She wanted to be an American.

By night the businesswoman was transformed into a glamour queen. She discovered the soft-lit world of cocktail lounges, and Turkish baths for the night—to "freshen up." And she spent more and more nights away from home. As she prepared for her evenings out, she often asked my advice about whether to wear the shocking-pink satin strapless with the fishtail pleat and the dyed-to-match shoes whose stiletto heels were ablaze with rhinestones, or the royal blue brocade with blue-tinted stockings, or the black dotted Swiss for simplicity's sake. I chose the pink. I began to draw pictures of pretty ladies in dresses, to design new ideas to win my mother's approval. She approved of the designs, but not of the fact that I was doing them.

I was doing everything wrong. Boys shouldn't talk with their hands. Boys don't sway their hips when they walk. (Remember what happened to Arthur?) Boys don't laugh at such a high pitch. I shouldn't laugh the way that was natural to me. It didn't sound natural.

Learned laughs don't come from the belly. Now, except for an occasional foray into camping, my walk, my talk, my laugh are all "acceptable." I learned well. I was always a good student, the teacher's pet, hugged with embarrassing approval in front of the whole class, bringing home honor certificates and report cards heavy with A's. But I wasn't learning something right. I wasn't learning how to be a "man." More drastic measures were needed for that.

First she tried hormone shots. The excuse was that I was too short, and I didn't want to grow up to be a runt like my father, did I? A year of weekly injections produced an excess of hormones that might have put a little more hair on my chest, but it didn't stop me from being attracted to hairy chests on other men. Maybe its main effect was to help me go bald earlier than anyone in the family.

Next came the manly art of violence: boxing lessons. I had to go to a gym in downtown Newark once a week and grapple with medicine balls and punching bags. Mainly I learned how to watch my eyes in the locker room. I couldn't seem to keep them on the locker. I was more interested in hugging my partners than in sparring with them anyway, but I wasn't completely aware of that yet. I didn't even know such things ever actually happened. Nor did I know there was a final exam in the self-defense course. Twice, in the street, coming home from Cub Scout meetings, friends would stop a perfectly amiable conversation and punch me in the mouth. I would fight back the best I could—not the way I had been taught, but by hitting them with the pile of music I was carrying from my piano lesson, or trying to turn the attack into a wrestling match. Days would go by with me still wondering what had provoked my friends into such outrages. Friends were few but deep, especially with the neighborhood crowd out of reach (hopefully). Finally they would explain that my mother had asked them to attack me for my own good. Thanks, Mom.

The guaranteed method was a summer of manly company for models and sports for training, with a little naure lore on the side. My mother made like Betsy Ross with the name tags and filled a trunk with shirts and socks and shorts all neatly labeled. I, meanwhile, went to the library and took out a pile of books for the summer, mainly animal adventure novels starring dogs with names like Lad or Awol and horses called Misty of Black Beauty. I carefully unpacked a third of the trunk and replaced my changes of athletic clothes with enough material to escape from my forced vacation, and off I went to the land of men: Kamp Kiamesha.

Sunday mornings we rose from our canvas-walled bunkhouses, where the bed wetters got the upper bunks as if by plan, and we were herded off to the canteen to draw a dime from our snack money to deposit as choiceless charity in the offering tray of the tidily nondenominational church. It seemed patently Protestant to me. The one denomination it was most definitely not was my forefathers' Judaism. Mother had dutifully warned me not to listen too hard, which was easy enough advice to follow, and so Sundays hardly fazed me. But she didn't warn me about the counselor who was always threatening to pin me down and make me smell his armpits and accept the used chewing gum from his mouth into mine. It was as close as I could get to nuzzling and kissing him, and I loved even the idea of it. In fact, I was probably the first to suggest it, and I did everything I could to encourage him. I don't remember a word of the Sunday morning sermons, but I remember exactly how good that chewing gum tasted.

Sunday afternoons my parents would be the very last to arrive after my father had put in his half a day at the grocery and had chugged Grandpa Simon's old Packard convertible out to the wilds of northern New Jersey. By the time they got there it was almost time for them to go, and I barely had the opportunity to show them the plastic lanyard I had laboriously braided to hold my house key around my neck, or the leather belt I had looped for my father. But in the brief while they were there, my mother had a chance to nose around and discover that I had been sneaking off to read in the woods instead of playing baseball, and she instructed the counselor with a five-dollar bill that it was going to be baseball, not books.

Mainly I spent my baseball time trying to convince everybody that it was going to rain any second and we'd better put away our gloves and go inside, while hoping fervently that no fly ball would find its way to my part of the outfield. My mother boasted enough of my professional boxing lessons to get me enrolled in the camp boxing contest, but I conceded that match by holding my bent elbows in front of my face and retreating. I have enough trouble hitting people I don't like, let alone people I don't even know. Also, I was scared.

Swimming wasn't much better. I nearly drowned because I was so entranced with the counselors' cocks bobbing blithely up and down as they tested the diving board. But hiking was the most trying: being the last to reach the mountaintop where we camped out overnight amid grizzlybear campfire stories and marshmallows toasted on sticks, and then to sleep on the bare rock top which gave the mountain its name of "Old Baldy," at whose base I awoke surprised in the morning, having slid there in my sleep. I trailed into camp an hour after everyone else that afternoon, my sneakers flopping because I had used their laces to tie my blanket together after I had lost the rope and my belt as well, causing my pants to droop around my hips, which were already beginning to itch from the poison ivy I had slept in. I lasted most of the summer. But even though I left early, I learned how to brew sassafras tea and what a salamander is, which contributed to a felt letter *K* for Kiamesha to sew on my sweater. I was kind of proud of the *K,* and I don't mind at all knowing about salamanders, even if I've never met one in Manhattan. And that chewing gum was some of the best chewing gum I've ever chewed.

I had my first erection when I was about twelve. I was riding my bicycle, bedecked with its colored handlebar streamers, bobbing plastic bird and Tab Hunter decal on the rear fender. Maybe the bicycle seat activated the hard-on, or maybe it was just time. I had no idea what it was about, not having had such delicate topics discussed with me in so many words. All I knew was that I liked it better when it was bigger, and I hoped it would be bigger the next time I went to see the family doctor, who was the only one left who still saw me naked. But it didn't take me long to figure out that a man is supposed to be ashamed if a bulge of desire can be seen in his pants. It's not civilized. And if the bulge should point at another man, it's not safe.

I began my forays into adolescent sexual experimentation just before I was thirteen. Like most boys that age, I started playing around with my friends. It started with after-school visits. Just school chums horsing around and all that. I'll show you mine if you'll show me yours. "Boys can see boys" (a motto of the public urinal). How about a little strip poker? Want to see my mother's diaphragm? How about my father's jockstrap? Let me see your dirty pictures (half a deck of straight porno playing cards). Why don't we try this position out? I proffered half the invitations and accepted the other half. But I hadn't yet had my first orgasm, and watching a friend masturbate was an illumination of the first order. The "white pee-pee" my mother had told me about hadn't prepared me for the beauty of a seemingly endless fountain of pearly semen spurting from the head of his cock. There was something sacred about it. It was only a matter of weeks until I could produce my own, and as soon as I learned what it felt like to come, I was hooked. I came whenever I could.

One afternoon I had a friend over, and we had the house to ourselves. We started out doing homework together, and it wasn't long before we were touching and looking interested in each other. Of course, just making love was out of the question, since we were all-American Jewish boys, so we had to find an excuse.

"Want to wrestle?" he challenged. Now there was a new angle.

"Sure," I murmured.

"What'll we wrestle for?"

"What do you mean, 'for'?" I was willing to yield to his strength with a minimum of struggle.

"There has to be a prize for the winner."

I was beginning to catch on. The prize was each other. "Suppose we do it like strip poker. The loser has to take something off after each round," I suggested, wanting to increase the skin contact as much as possible.

We wrestled for match after match, yielding and overcoming with ease, first one then the other, and with each match a shoe or a shirt or a pair of pants was quickly discarded until we were in our underwear, and soon out of it and trying out the delights of "69" without knowing they had a name, and having a frighteningly wonderful time, even if it was forbidden, lost in delight, until I heard the sound of the key turning in the lock. My mother was home!

"Arnold?" she called.

In the minute it took for her to cross the apartment from the front door to the door to my room, we hastily abandoned our passion and scrambled into our pants. We were just zipping up when she appeared in the doorway, a look of stark horror painted on her face.

"What are you two *doing?*" she sputtered.

"Hi, Mom. Oh, we were just wrestling," I lied guiltily.

She wasn't buying. "I think you'd better go home now," she told my friend. "It's suppertime . . . and I don't think you should visit Arnold anymore." He collected himself and fled. Then came the inquisition.

"Arnold, what were you doing with him?"

"I told you, Mom, just wrestling."

"Now remember, just tell me the truth, and you won't be punished. What do you mean, 'wrestling'?"

"You know, wrestling," I insisted, my voice quivering with guilt.

"Did you *touch* each other?" She filled the word with obscenity.

"Of course we touched each other. We were wrestling. I told you." My voice was sinking to a whisper. I was starting to sweat.

"Did you touch each other anywhere you shouldn't? Your private parts?"

Evasion was no longer possible. "Just a feel," I said as casually as I could, to minimize the indictment.

"Just a feel," she echoed. Her voice dripped with doom. She knew! Would she tell? Would she tell my father? The school? The police?

But nothing happened. Nothing for a week. I thought it was over, until one morning when she told me to take a bath and put on clean underwear.

"What for?" I asked, groaning.

"You're going to the doctor."

"But I'm not sick," I protested.

"We'll see about that," she warned. "Now hurry up and get washed." I knew what it was about then.

We traveled all the way to Lakewood, where her sister knew a good physician. She couldn't bring this disgrace to our own family doctor. Doom hovered above my head. I felt like Norma Shearer in a wooden cart being scorned all the way to the guillotine. The heroine within me quaked.

The doctor asked lots of questions as he weighed and measured me and did the usual prodding and pinching and poking. I told him everything, determined to make a clean breast of it and be cured, contrite before my confessor even if I wasn't a Catholic, desperate to regain my mother's respect, so I could reenter the lists and joust for her love. Finally he called her in and delivered his verdict: "Your son is normal," he said. "He's just been experimenting in the ways boys his age all do. And don't worry about the other symptoms you told me about." I threw her a sidelong glance. I knew what symptoms he meant: my walk, my talk, my laugh. He finished, "Do you want him to be a street-corner hooligan? He's sensitive and intelligent. All boys aren't ruffians."

I wanted to kiss that doctor, but that would have deflated my new image as a heterosexual aesthete. Escapes can be just so narrow, and I was going to let this sleeping dog lie even if it took a sledgehammer.

"Thank you, Doctor," she said. There was a note of tentative relief in her voice, perhaps a willingness to accept what she knew wasn't true, even if it meant lying to herself. My mother could use her fancy as well as she could rationalize. Who was she to question medical science? Her son was a heterosexual.

As soon as we got to the curb, she turned to me and asked, "Did he measure your penis to see if it was normal?"

It took a lot of years before I got around to surveying other guys' hard-ons to find out that mine is normal. I spent those years trying my damnedest to be straight.

2

"TODAY I AM A MAN." I WASN'T SURE THE CONGREGA-
tion at my Bar Mitzvah would have agreed if they could
have seen my dreams, but to all outward appearances
everything was fine. As a Jew, I knew the entire ceremony was a sham. Being Jewish for my mother was
largely a matter of getting dressed up on the High Holy
Days and standing in a mink stole on the synagogue
steps. For my father it was sneaking away from the
Yom Kippur fast to have jelly doughnuts. (We hid the
leftovers behind a tree before we went back to the
temple.) Eventually it became "Say a prayer for me."
And finally none of us went. I had quit Hebrew school
after only one season, and my parents had hired a
rabbi to teach me to read my Bar Mitzvah passage from
the Torah phonetically. I didn't have the faintest idea
what I was talking about as I chanted, *"Bawrachoo ess
Adonai . . ."* and it came as no surprise to me when
an aged member of the synagogue rose to his infirm
height and denounced me as a false Jew. I felt like a
false man, a false Jew, a false everything. Guilt. The
rest was kissing aunts and checks in envelopes (and not

one traditional fountain pen); the rest is old photographs. I have never felt quite comfortable in a synagogue since that day.

Home was no more comfortable than *schul* even when my mother decided to sell the Mapes Avenue house. It was the first house on the block to go to a black family. If I was threatened with a little roughing up while I actually lived on Mapes Avenue, my life was in real peril if I ever dared to show my face there once we had moved only a few blocks away to Renner Avenue. The great relief I felt at being away from the daily clutches of Sonny and Paul was shattered by the wrathful phone calls that didn't let up for weeks, day and night.

"Hello?"

"Is your mother home?"

"No. Can I take a message?"

"Yes. When she comes home, tell her she's a fucking nigger-loving bitch, and better she should live with the *shvartzers* than me. Tell her. . . ."

I hung up. We had the number changed, and the new one was unlisted.

Though it was only a few blocks, my mother noted that while everyone who was going up in the world was moving southward, deeper into Newark's Weequahic section, from the heart of which one might penetrate finally to the suburbs, we were moving northward, closer to where we had begun. We were in a third-floor walk-up again. My father was failing her dream. A lock soon appeared on the bedroom door, and my father fashioned his own lair in the sun parlor at the other end of the flat.

"My mom and dad went out for a drink the other night," one of the boys on the block told my horrified ears, "and they saw your mother out with another man."

"Business," she offered bluntly as explanation when

I asked. I treated her sex life the way she treated mine. I did my best to shrug it off and went about the business of beginning high school.

In the first year at Weequahic High we were given the latest aid that science had bestowed upon education, the Kuder Preference Test. Each question was a list of things to do, and we had to choose our favorites. When the list included "building a house," I thought back to the fumbling failures of woodworking I had produced in grammar-school manual-training class. If it included "drawing a picture," I remembered my flair for fashion. By the time I finished, preferring picture drawing to house building, my tastes had declared that I should become a clerk in an art store. It wasn't what I wanted to be. I didn't know what I wanted to be.

"Never mind," my mother said with classic finality. "You're going to be a doctor."

More than 90 percent of Weequahic's inmates were in training for the American Jewish dream. The population of the school was sparsely peppered with a few black and white Christians, who were regarded more as pets than as threats, and a few intellectuals, who were regarded as out of it. Inside, I felt in the latter category, creepy because I was bright. Guys weren't supposed to be bright. If they were, they hid it. Outside, I did my best to look like the rest. We wore chino pants with buckles stretched (I tried not to notice how appealingly) tight across the ass. Dungarees weren't allowed, and narrow pegged pants were for South Side High, which was in a different section of town, where the *goyim* were. The girls wore long, tight skirts, with slits or pleats to allow for the possibility of walking, or the opposite extreme of voluminous hoop skirts, which made boarding the #14 bus a precarious challenge.

Our teams won lots of trophies, except for the foot-

ball team, whose future surgeons' hands were kept out
of such danger by threats from home. I wasn't into
sports at all, so there was no problem for me, much
to my mother's dismay. The girls provided a land office
business for the local beauty parlors, and if their careful coiffures were impaired in girls' gym class, tears
were known to flow. I stayed safely among them. We
ate huge kosher hot dogs at lunch in Sid's and danced
the lindy and the bunnyhop, my friends' angora pom-
poms dangling from their detachable collars in time to
the rock 'n' roll and bouncing on the equally detachable
foam-rubber falsies they wore beneath their sweaters
to amplify their charms. Every fall several of them
would show up with shorter, straighter noses, usually
modeled after Debbie Reynolds' all-American perk.
Boys generally kept the noses they had been provided
with. Our looks weren't as important as whether we
could make a living.

I wore my hair in a Chicago box, long on the sides
and short on the top, with a precisely casual curl jut-
ting out over my forehead, the entirety plastered into
place with setting gel, so that only a determined rake
could get through. The non-Jewish adolescent boys
my mother called *shkutsim* wore sideburns, Elvis Pres-
ley greaser style, definitely not collegiate-looking. And
their female counterparts, the *shickses,* wore scuffed
ballerina slippers and shoulder bags and chewed gum.
Weequahic's version of the gang was the clique, the
social club, the fraternity, none of which I was interested in joining. Being too close to "the guys" could
expose secret dreams even I didn't want to see. In a
clique one could get points for owning a mohair suit or
having a summer membership in a swim club or, for
the girls, throwing the most expensive Sweet Sixteen
party, featuring the right people and a large corsage
sprouting sugar cubes affixed with colored pipe cleaners

by some hyperthyroid florist. I was amiable, but I watched as if from afar as they all led their lives. Deep inside me lived someone who wasn't the person they thought they knew, the one about whom they wrote in the yearbook, "A cheerful youth, courteous and kind; a steady friend with an energetic mind."

My best friend was Leslie Berger. We could talk about what the girls were wearing, how debasing it was to ask for a date, how bushy the class president's eyebrows were, how tight the track star's pants were in the back, and how embarrasing gym was; but we were just buddies, the intellectual sort, not those street-corner hooligans. Ours was a friendship of aesthetes. We loved Rachmaninoff and complained to each other about our mothers.

Not surprisingly, my mother hated Leslie. She much preferred my other friends, like Gerry Beatty, the ones who weren't suspiciously weird or withdrawn or otherwise unwholesome, the ones who later invited me to their weddings as usher or best man.

When I reached fifteen, my parents' marriage reached an end. We left my father alone on Renner Avenue and moved to a garden apartment in Elizabeth. He had the legal right to visit us on weekends, but he didn't exercise it. Occasionally I would see him back in Newark, where he worked at driving a delivery truck, having lost his grocery to bankruptcy. There, one night on the street, he spoke to me of love for the first time in my life.

"Your mother is the only woman I'll ever love," he announced melodramatically. I looked at him suspiciously. I had heard that sort of talk in the movies, but never at home.

"I'm sorry," I offered.

He grew portentous, glad to have an outlet for his long-pent emotions. "I'm a one-woman man. She'll find someone else, but I'll be true to her." I didn't tell him she had already found someone else, sometime before she left him. It was hard to care about his feelings, hard to believe he even had any, since I'd never seen them before. Perhaps it was a great moment in our lives, but I felt it had come too late for everyone concerned. He continued, his tone turning sour, "I guess I just couldn't satisfy her, you understand. She needs big cars and fancy clothes and mansions. A real home wasn't good enough for her. She called me a failure, but I did my best. Am I right?"

"Yes, Dad," I said, placating. "You did your best."

He looked at me for a long time. I wondered if maybe he were seeing me for once, not just a stranger with the title of Son, but me, a person, someone he hadn't ever thought of knowing before. Then his brow grew furrowed, and his bright blue eyes turned to ice.

"Let me tell you something," he stormed. "This marriage would still be alive: I would still be with the woman I love if it weren't for you. You're my son; you were there. It was up to you to defend me when I was attacked. It's your fault!"

I couldn't believe what I had just heard. I was sorry for his sadness. I knew he was lashing out blindly to assuage a mortal wound. I knew he couldn't mean what he'd said, but didn't he know that my sense of security and love was also staggering from the blows it was being dealt?

"You were supposed to teach *me* how to live," I screamed. "You were supposed to defend *me*. How can I take on your responsibilities? *You're* supposed to be the father, not me!"

There followed months of silence between us, but eventually we managed an occasional visit. I could go to his house even if he couldn't come to ours.

My mother decorated the new apartment with a ven-

geance to make up for the battered furniture she had
endured since she had first been married. There were
barnacles of experience covering the starry-eyed sixteen-
year-old girl who had opened the dry-cleaning shop,
but the dreams weren't buried far below the surface.
It would simply take a more indirect route to reach
success, and more determination. She baited her hook
with care. The living room sported a seventeen-foot
custom-made couch, L-shaped in bright yellow and
covered with plastic to preserve it. A kidney-shaped
piece of glass topped a gilded driftwood coffee table
into which plastic leaves and bisque figurines were set
in random profusion. The rug was white, at least beneath the plastic runners that ran from doorway to
doorway, the rest turning rapidly gray. The dining table
was a large slab of inch-thick glass set on a curlicued
extravaganza of white wrought iron and surrounded by
similarly white chairs bedecked with shocking pink
cushions, which matched the upholstery on the living-
room armchair. The kitchen was so pink it seemed hard
to breathe in it. Even the cabinets and the refrigerator
were sprayed in pale pastel above a pink tile floor, so
that to find a snack we had to wade through a sea of
cotton candy. The hallway was lined with newly an-
tiqued planters, spurting a miniature rain forest of
plastic greenery and crowned on the wall above by a
pair of bisque shepherds piping unheard melodies to
bisque maidens mounted on velvet. Her bedroom was
done in lavender, resplendent with mirrors, huge
dressers cluttered with perfume bottles, the favorite
being Shalimar, which filled the air with a heavy, in-
scrutable sweetness for an hour after she got dressed.
The room starred a king-sized bed with a lavender
brocade headboard and a bedspread made to match.
A fragile collection of bisque people over-populated the
wall above it.

My brother and I shared a bedroom crammed with matching beds and dressers with desks on top of them. The only taste other than my mother's was expressed on the wall over my bed, where I had hung large posters featuring a bullfighter who had been poured into his pants, a street in Paris notable for *not* being a northern New Jersey scene, and two reproductions: one a wistful head by Modigliani and the other a whimsical head by Paul Klee. It was the Klee that bothered my mother most. It spoiled the whole apartment in her eyes and saved it in mine. Once I came home just in time to find her ripping it from the wall. I rushed to save it, pushing her away in the process. For days I was plastered with enough guilt to convince me I had attempted matricide. But the Klee stayed up.

The source of all this earthly abundance was Frank Granucci, a sweet, blunt man who had gone to the third grade and abandoned the refinements of education, preferring to make his living from the numbers rackets, furtively meeting shady characters in the dead of night, exchanging slips of numbers and wads of money. He had a low-slung, full face topped with a low forehead and a tough but not unkind look in his small brown eyes. He wore shiny suits and silk ties with white-on-white shirts that boasted monogrammed cuffs or pockets and diamond cuff links that vied with his sapphire pinky rings. He had no hobbies other than an occasional game of solitaire, no interests, and no friends. But he did have one drawback: a wife.

My mother plotted and schemed to take him from his wife with the sort of astuteness that brought Elizabeth Taylor to beloved infamy. His wife, as I heard it, was a frump, and my mother did all she could to represent her opposite: the perfect blend of glamour, class, and domesticity. He had no children of his own, so my brother and I were presented as his vicarious posterity, with the fact that a hysterectomy had left her unable to bear further children left carefully blurred. And of course the hair of metallic gold was sworn to be natural. ("Well, it *was* much lighter when I was a little girl," she rationalized to me.) There was an ethnic wrinkle in the affair, since she had no special fondness for Italians, and he was given to comments like "If everybody hates da Jews, there must be a reason. Didn't they kill God?" But he wasn't especially religious, and she smoothed it over with a few spotty references to the glory of Italian opera and a lot of olive oil on the pasta dishes in whose preparation she had become an overnight expert. Why fight? We could have the best of both worlds. At Rosh Hashanah, the Jewish New Year, she produced a four-foot-long loaf of braided egg bread and announced that she had baked the *challah* herself, though it wouldn't take an expert in Yiddish culture to figure out that no more than two-thirds of it could possibly have fit into the oven in our pink kitchen. And at Christmas we had a white paper treelet, studded with paper roses that matched the shocking pink upholstery, each one harboring a tiny red light glittering in its heart.

That was when I got my chance to be my mother's knight, and the price was merely my own morality. Would I call Frank's wife and tell her she had competition, so she would turn into a shrew and alienate him? Nope. Would I take a revealing letter and tuck it into her mailbox bereft of postmark? She had done as much for a friend once. But I wouldn't do as much for my own mother, ungrateful wretch that I was. Would I at least talk to Frank, threaten to leave home if he continued to subject my household to such disgrace? That much I would do.

She carefully arranged to leave us alone in the house together at a propitious moment, and I interrupted his reading of the New York *Daily News* with a little dose of our own tabloid reality.

"Ahem . . . Frank, is it all right if I talk to you for a minute?"

"Sure, kid, what's bodderin' ya?"

"It's my mother. I'm ashamed even in front of the neighbors. They all know you come in and out of here at all hours, and they know she's a divorcee. I'm worried about her reputation."

"You know I really think a lot of your mother," he offered.

"Then why do you make a prostitute out of her?" I challenged. Sometimes life was almost as good as the movies.

"Your mother ain't no hoor," he defended. "She's a lady."

"A lady doesn't have to be ashamed of what she does. A lady doesn't have to worry about her children's future because of her past. What's going to happen to me and Ira if this keeps up? I'll have to leave here if I'm going to be a professional man. I can't afford such scandal." My absurd hypocrisy was not lost on me, but I knew I was appealing to his morality. I managed to keep a straight face, burying my urge to giggle beneath an outpour of righteous wrath.

"I didn't think of it that way," he confessed.

"Besides"— I frosted my cake—"we like having you around, not just at night but all the time. We want to be a family." I didn't actually mind having him around, but I had little hope of becoming any sort of family. It was just that I knew a thing or two about fathers.

As soon as he completed his quickie Mexican divorce, ignoring the strictures of New Jersey and the Catholic Church, they honeymooned in Acapulco and were married in Maryland on the way back. I had a new stepfather, my mother a new breadwinner, and Frank a new name. She convinced him to change Granucci to Granger. It was more American. Ann Granger was much more American than Hannah Brockoff had even dreamed of being.

In spite of our new-found wealth, I sought a degree of independence by working part-time at a series of jobs. Whether I was delivering a huge, heavy mailbag of lawyers' contracts in downtown Newark or wrapping packages in a men's clothing store, selling layaway Christmas toys to Newark's poor in a store in the heart of the black ghetto or being a copyboy in the Newark *Evening News* sports department, I found myself in the company of men who talked endlessly about one subject: sex. At least to them it was sex. To me it was heterosexuality, but surrounded by "Check that chick's knockers," and "Boy, could I go for a piece of that ass," I kept my definitions to myself, managing to evade, to equivocate, to acquiesce, and to be thankful no one could read my secret mind.

For five summers I worked for one of my mother's sisters and her husband in their five-and-ten-cent store in Seaside Heights, New Jersey. My eleven-hour workdays were spent cajoling elderly Italian ladies in pedal pushers to buy religious pictures laminated onto slabs of wood, sweeping floors and straightening piles of clothes, looking for the plastic button to match the missing one on a housedress, and, when I could find a few free moments, quietly reading the Brontës and Walt Whitman in the corner. I also began to read books about men who loved men and women who loved women, books that invariably ended in misery and death, heroes and heroines who walked into the sea or died in motorcycle crashes or at the very least ended up alone and unwanted. But I hid those books while I was reading them and threw them away as soon as I was done.

In the evenings I taught myself to smoke cigarettes and walked the boardwalk alone. It was lined with pizza stands and children's rides and brightly lighted wheels of chance offering caged parakeets and stuffed animals and other, not so tempting prizes. There was temptation on the boardwalk though, in the handsome dark young men in their white undershirts, their sunbronzed, muscled arms around the waists of girls who wore lots of makeup and sailor caps turned inside out, bucket style, on their heads. I tried to be attracted to the girls' legs in their shorts, but it was always their boyfriends' hairy chests that drew me, their white smiles and easy masculinity, even the arrogance they affected, putting on their image of the Fifties stud, the "greaser," with a grace I could never aspire to in my horn-rimmed glasses and my pudgy shape.

As much as I wanted to be straight, it was always the images of those men who turned me on as I masturbated in secret. It was the hints of splendor I caught in outlines and bulges, in men's-room glimpses and flashes on the beach, where I eyed the promise of full crotches in brief swimsuits, staring as long as possible without danger of detection, hoping for a sudden motion or a raised leg to expose a glimpse of testicle. I knew who was and who wasn't wearing a jockstrap. I waited at the water's edge for eternities, for the guy in the white bathing suit to emerge, just to see if there might be the shadow of a cockhead or the cleft of his buttocks revealed by the wetness. My fantasies didn't travel too much further. In those days I could masturbate to memories of carelessly exposed jockstrap waistbands. Once in a while a breathtaking vision of manhood would come into the store and try on a bathing suit. If he rejected it, I would wait for my chance as soon as possible after he left and feel the crotch for any traces of his body's warmth, sometimes even locking myself in the bathroom to effect a furtive orgasm.

I kept all that to myself. Socially, I was a heterosexual. During the school year I escorted the daughters of Newark to movies and bowling alleys and restaurants, to dances and hops and proms. Every date was ended with interminable tongue kissing in the back hallway. I don't know if my attentions turned my dates on, but they didn't do too much for me. It was just that I knew everyone else did it, and there had to be something to brag about the next day; but I couldn't escape the feeling that I wasn't the only one for whom it was done out of obligation rather than desire. Whatever their reasons, everybody was pretending to have a good time. We were all afraid not to: it would have seemed un-American.

Through all the charade, there remained the men I looked at out of the corner of my eye, the men I dreamed about with firm jaws and wide shoulders and hirsute torsos and pedulous cocks, the heroic individualism of James Dean, the beauty of Paul Newman. I locked their images away in a secret place I tried not to examine. It was like owning a Pandora's box. And I tried to turn my attention to studies or skirts or sleep when they invaded my terrified fantasy life, for fear they would betray me. I went alone to see *Tea and Sympathy,* which showed the scorn reserved for anyone even suspected of being "queer." But the public sees only what it's been trained to. When I went out with my mother, I looking older than my mid-teens, she looking younger than her mid-thirties, people would inevitably stare at us curiously, as if we were a strange couple—perhaps a wealthy matron and a too-young gigolo. Motherhood was never a matter of apple pies for us. It was more a matter of seduction, if my deepest dreams meant anything. She was one woman who turned me on, though I couldn't confess it to myself, let alone to her. So she dealt with my incestuous fantasies unwittingly as she dealt with those of the people who stared at us in restaurants. "It's all right," she would call cheerily across several crowded tables. "He's my son." But it wasn't all right. It made me want to crawl under the linoleum.

College was a more serious problem. In college people had sex. The Fabulous Fifties and their hypocrisy were drawing to a merciful close as I entered Rutgers-Newark, refusing to stray too far from the home I could hardly endure. But the new sexual freedoms I found seemed to me like more links in the same old chain. It took a little more cunning to keep my closet door intact through those years when my female classmates sought entry, but I had new devices at my command. I was being educated.

Rutgers-Newark housed a diverse crowd in an ill-assorted collection of converted office buildings, breweries, and factories scattered around Washington Park in the downtown shopping district. The fraternity types were throwing loud beer parties and bragging about their sexual conquests. The theater and newspaper and yearbook crowds I hung around with were having affairs with each other, musical-beds style, and coping with the consequences of recrimination and abortion and guilt. I started with a major in pre-med, but I began to change in ways I couldn't have anticipated. I opened to new ideas that high school had kept me sheltered from, new perspectives on myself and on history that began to free me from my past. I gave up any pretense to religion, already angry at the Judaism I felt alien to, and I became a vociferous atheist.

Yet, riding home on a bus through the dreary towns of northern New Jersey one evening, in a startling change that lasted perhaps moments, perhaps longer, the world seemed utterly different to me, transfigured. (It was years before terms like "psychedelic" and "expanded consciousness" were part of the popular vocabulary, and I had never so much as sampled a joint.) A glow descended over me, and everything I saw was beautiful, meaningful, in some new way *right*. I passed slums that I had earlier related to only sociologically. They still sagged with their own grayness. The garbage was still strewn at the bases of its rusted containers. Everything was as usual. But I saw it with a brilliant clarity that no optometrist's efforts could account for. Each individual thing seemed beautiful precisely because it was whatever it was. Everything radiated the perfection of being real, as if I were seeing it all for the first time in its true form, as if a veiled curtain had been ripped aside. Things remained their separate selves, but each thing fused into its neighbors, and the relationship of everything into one vast whole seemed obvious, a whole that stretched farther than the bus window could show me, but a whole that I knew with certainty was there. When I let my self-awareness relax for just a moment, I became a part of that whole. I felt wonderful. I felt larger than myself, but I didn't know what this was any more than I had known what my first erection was. They didn't teach this in school either.

The English teachers at Rutgers were a strange breed, given to Byronic affectations or Tennysonian pomposity, but they talked about the things that mattered to me: beauty and meaning, values, the sources and patterns of our culture's definitions in a perspective that revealed them all as mortal. There was something there for me in the poems and the discussions. There were more ideals for me in literature than there were in chemistry or calculus or scientific German; so I

changed my major to English, sloughing off "my son
the doctor" as someone else's skin and declaring shiny-
eyed independence. My mother announced I was
doomed to become an "Educated Nothing." But I had
my own ideas. I began to write poetry, at first senti-
mental and shy and clumsy, then swaying its style and
substance in each new intellectual wind that caught it:
T. S. Eliot, John Donne, e. e. cummings, Dylan
Thomas. I was an "English major" type, all right. I
even became editor of the literary magazine and president of the English Club, introducing polite lecturers
and sipping puce-colored punch. I didn't much relish
the effete side of academia. Upstairs from our apartment in Elizabeth lived a middle-aged college teacher,
a bachelor who kept cats and wore too many rings and
listened to Mozart with delicate delight. He frightened
me. He was what a gay English major might aspire to
be, but I dreamed of more. In spite of my affinity for
Mozart and cats and rings, I wanted to be something
different. I imagined myself an Israeli *kibbutznik,* my
tanned elbow leaning on a hoe in the Middle Eastern
sun, living communally, fighting for freedom, like Sal
Mineo in *Exodus.*

But that implied physical exercise, and gym, for me,
was the pits. It was a world where I didn't belong.
I gritted my teeth through the locker room, trying to
keep my eyes glued to my clothes, changing swiftly,
helplessly darting peripheral glances at precisely the
moment between the taking off of someone's pants and
his turning to hang them up, when the corner of my
eye told me an ass or a cock might be glimpsed bare.
The whole thing was nothing to them. They were
oblivious. But it certainly wasn't delight for me. It was
sheer terror. Men don't like being looked at the way
they look at women: for their bodies. If I gave myself
away it could cause violence. The violence of games

like Bombardment only made it worse. Somehow I always ended up alone, having discreetly stayed behind while the rest of my team was pelted out of the game with a stinging hail of volleyballs. It was a moment of exquisite fear, standing alone waiting for the onslaught, trying not to flinch, like the biblical adultress waiting to be stoned. It was a masochist's moment. I usually chose to go swimming instead, but while that bared the asses of my classmates, it also bared my inevitable reaction to them, and I was afraid if they saw it, I'd wish I'd chosen Bombardment.

Leslie remained my closest friend in college. We shared many classes together. During lunch hours we would sit in Washington Park in front of the school and, surrounded by the traffic noise of downtown Newark, we would figure out bicycle routes across the maps on the inside covers of our European history books. Both of us wanted to escape. I wanted to see what lay across the ocean, but secretly I was afraid of being lost in a strange place where I didn't know the language. We remained park-bench explorers.

But college wasn't all an ivory tower. While I was there, the apathetic Silent Generation of the Eisenhower years awakened into the dreams of the Kennedy era, and I found myself with a social conscience and a picket sign in my hand.

The issue was racism. I joined the NAACP, a radical move in the pre-Panther days; and I drew posters of black hands shaking white hands across a sea of brotherhood. When the first sit-ins happened at Woolworth's lunch counters in the South, we decided to bring the issue home by picketing Woolworth's on Broad and Market Streets, the concrete heart of Newark. We were afraid. Picketing had something to do with strikes and Communists. But this was a question of morals. We were doing the right thing, acting on our beliefs. Yet for all our pains we were ignored by blacks and whites alike.

When I got home, I was greeted with the white backlash.

"Where were you today?" she wanted to know.

"At school." I offered some of the truth.

"Don't lie to me," the ranting began. "Your father's sister saw you carrying signs with a bunch of *shvartzers* at Broad and Market streets. He called up and told me the whole story."

"We were picketing for the Negroes' right to eat where they please," I asserted.

"What do the jigs have to do wit' you?" my stepfather chimed in.

"Don't chime in," my mother said to him and, turning to me in the same breath, went on, "what were you doing?" She sounded as if she had caught me in the bedroom with my pants down again.

"We were only showing sympathy by boycotting—"

"Who's 'we'?" she demanded.

"I belong to the NAACP at school. There are lots of people in it."

"White people?" she said, sneering, in the same tone in which she had asked me how many boys and how many girls I had played with on a childhood afternoon.

But I was no longer a child. "White people with consciences," I snapped.

"Why don't you let them fight their own battles?" tried my stepfather. "Or are they too busy collecting welfare checks?"

"What about the people you sold the Mapes Avenue house to?" I darted at my mother.

"I learned a lot from them," she screamed. "Think what you want to, but you're not parading around in the streets with signs where my friends can see you. It's bad for my business!"

"People have a right to be free," I shouted.

We went on until four in the morning at a Wagnerian pitch, until we were exhausted. Finally she said with determination. "If I hear of you doing anything like this again, you're leaving this house. I won't support a troublemaker under my roof. I mean it."

I was equally determined, so I increased the secrecy necessary to do what I believed in, and with it I increased the distance between myself and the people I lived with. I went about my own business, coming home only to sleep. If I came home very late, she would be awake in her room, smoking, claiming to be worried about me. If I got up early to type a term paper, with the typewriter muffled on a crumpled towel, she was awake, smoking, annoyed by me. I was supposed to be guilty, but I was beginning to be angry instead. I spent more and more time at school.

I met Renee Weissberg in the college newspaper office. She was as feature perfect as Elizabeth Taylor, including the darkly limpid eyes and the raven tresses. But she was billowingly overweight. She was only sixteen, but bright enough to be in college. She was sorely in need of love, ignored by her mother and castigated by her stepfather for being a whore, her only sin being utter innocence. She was a latter-day Isadora Duncan, or perhaps an early flower child, wearing ropes of pearls around her waist and fresh roses in her hair, their scent obscured by the musky perfumes she affected. She sent me butterfly wings in the mail.

For all her pains I gave her only grief by trying to be what I was not. She called me in the middle of the night, sent me long, tear-stained letters, groped me as I was driving my mother's Cadillac, hatched plots to get me to marry her. Though the real thing we shared was a sophomoric self-pity about our lives at home, she insisted on seeing me as her knight. Well, the lance was limp when she finally got me into bed. I felt a total failure. She took it as a rejection of her female charms and wept, and then she became angry. Our relationship turned into one prolonged fight, until her final remark. "Keep your precious semen. I don't want it anyway."

Still undaunted, I went on trying harder to want women, and to ignore the growing magnetism of men. The longest affair I had was with Esther Schwartz. She had a plain face and long dark hair. She was an artist, and we enjoyed each other's creativity. We saw each other for over a year: a date at a dance, coffee in the student lounge, movies, parties, walks in the park, long good-night kisses in the car parked in front of her house. As time went on I was encouraged into bold- ness, allowing the good-night kisses to develop into fondling and fingering. We carried on and on, but we never seemed to go as far as I thought I should want to. There was always a firm resistance when it came to pushing down the pants. I didn't know that "No, no, no" meant "Try a little harder," but I tried harder any- way. I brought her flowers and took her out to dinner and then home to my bedroom, right past my news- paper-absorbed stepfather and into the arms of failure.

But I tried harder still, back at her house, and finally got it to work. It was functioning, even if it wasn't my idea of fun. But my noble experiment was shattered when I, of all people, was mistaken for Don Juan.

One night we were at her house, studying together. When the family had at last retired, we did too, up to her bedroom, for some extracurricular biology. We blithely turned out the light and hopped into bed, mind- less of its squeakings, mindless of my mother's larger- than-life Cadillac parked beneath her parents' bed- room window, until footsteps padded down the hallway, and a voice called, "Esther?" It was her father.

We scrambled out of bed and rushed madly about, colliding with each other in our haste. "I'm in my room, Dad," she answered.

"What are you doing in there?"

"Studying. Just studying." At that point we thought it might be nice to provide some evidence to that effect by turning on the light. The bulb chose that moment to burn out. Trapped!

I got my pants on, grabbed my shoes, stuffed my socks in my pocket, and ducked into the closet, reaching hastily out for my undershirt in Esther's hand and closing the door with all due silent speed. I was terrified. But somehow at the same time I wanted to roll on the floor with giggles. It couldn't be me this movie was happening to! It would probably make my mother happy if I were caught, erase the memory of her catching me with the wrong partner, even if she didn't like Esther, who thought her too bourgeois and wore black turtleneck sweaters like a beatnik.

Esther hopped back into bed and called out, "I'm going to bed now, Dad."

The Cadillac was sitting just outside his bedroom window. I wondered if he would notice. His footsteps padded back and forth. I wondered if he had a shotgun. I could hear him grumbling as he went back to his room. I could hear his bedsprings creak as he eased himself next to his sleeping wife. I waited. Finally Esther opened the door, and I sneaked silently home.

She called me before school the next morning. "I have to see you," she said. "My father thinks we should announce our engagement."

Engagement? I thought. Marriage? A family. A house. A permanent charade. Somebody else's life. A cage.

I met her that afternoon at school. "I've been thinking about our relationship," I said gently. "Are you sure we're suited to live together?" I played on every fear and doubt and twentieth-century anxiety I could. Somehow she convinced her father. Two years later she married a computer programmer.

I had tried.

I finally confessed to myself that I was a homosexual. I confessed to my best friend, Leslie, too. And he confessed to me. The same confession. We suffered the blow fate had dealt us in years of prolonged telephonings of mutual self-pity. We referred to our common vice by the code name "Peanut Butter," because there was a bar near school named Skippy's that was reputedly gay, even though we were both afraid of being seen there. Although we commiserated, we really felt contempt for each other's sexuality, because we saw disquieting reflections of ourselves in it. Ultimately I could no longer endure the waspishness we engendered in each other, and I asked him to stop calling.

He was the only homosexual friend I had until I was twenty-nine.

3

I DIDN'T HAVE SEX WITH A MAN UNTIL I WAS TWENTY and had just graduated from Rutgers. It happened in the romantic setting of the Port Authority bus terminal on my way back from looking for a job commensurate with my status as an Educated Nothing. Each day, after I spent the morning all over Manhattan, answering ads for editorial assistants, I spent the afternoon learning that the Port Authority building had a schedule of more than buses. It had a whole other life, and I proceeded to unravel its secrets.

I must have spent hours at the urinals, cautiously craning my neck to get a glimpse of cock, drying my hands with painstaking deliberation while trying to see what came tumbling out of the zippers reflected in the mirror above the sinks. It didn't take too long to figure out that most of the hustling went on downstairs in the main section and outside, around Forty-Second Street, and that most of the action went on not at the urinals but in the stalls. I could get a fair image of who was in which stall by looking through the slit between the door and the partition as if to see whether

55

the booth were occupied. (I always had such excuses made up to explain all my acts. I always pretended I was doing something legitimate, acting "as if," and I always felt slimy.)

It wasn't long before I was one of the men in the booths, my face a secret, making pirate's feet out of the feet in the next booth with the pants bunched up around the ankles and making lumberjack's eyes out of the eyes that peered in as if to see whether the booth were occupied. Once I saw the foot in the next stall begin to tap its toe, as if to some slow melody, silent but persistent. I'm not sure how I made the connection in my mind, but I answered with a silent tapping of my own, responding beat for beat. His foot edged closer. I followed his lead. Soon our shoes touched, but only long enough to establish contact. We didn't want to draw attention to ourselves. His fingertips appeared below the partition that separated us. I touched them. My fantasies blossomed. Soon a piece of toilet paper was proffered. I was confused, but when I opened it, I understood. Stationery! His note said that he worked in an office in the building, and we made arrangements to meet outside the men's room. He was a plain-looking man, nondescript, but my eyes easily anointed him into my Sir Lancelot.

I followed him deep into the recesses of the building, terrified. But I had dreamed of sucking a man's cock and clasping his buttocks, a modest enough aspiration that seemed the ultimate fulfillment to me, and no terror was going to stop me. I was intent on making love. I did, but as far as he was concerned, it was a blow job.

"It was my first time," I said sentimentally, as I departed.

"I hope we didn't leave any traces," he said. "I don't want my boss to find out."

His chewing gum had gotten stuck all over my pants, and I went back to New Jersey bearing it as a mark of Cain, sure all the commuters knew exactly what I had been doing.

Soon I became a habitué. I found a job for seventy dollars a week at Channel Five, writing advertisements for their rerun shows, such as "Stay tuned for action-packed adventure, next . . ." or "Channel Five brings you adventure-filled action tonight at nine." I usually spent half the day finishing my work, window-shopped the lunch hour away, and then wrote poems and did crossword puzzles for the afternoon. And every evening I stopped to study the Port Authority's subculture. Some men made a lifestyle of it, bringing suitcases with mirrored tops to see who was in the next stall, or shopping bags to hide their partners' feet so they could use the cubicle two at a time as ten-cent rent-a-rooms for sex. Some partitions even had "gloryholes" through which one might take a look and then insert a cock for sucking. Lust is very inventive. Its results were often bizarre, but it sure beat spending my time in Elizabeth, New Jersey.

Home was undergoing a transformation during that period. My mother had decided that she deserved better than a garden apartment and had begun the campaign that would lay the foundation of her dream castle. For all the time we had lived there, we had eaten on the glass-topped, curlicued extravaganza in the dining alcove. Suddenly we were eating on a tiny ice-cream table in the pink kitchen. We had to move it laboriously from its corner, lift it over the stove and into the center of the room before dinner, and replace it afterward. We ate with my elbow in the sink and my stepfather's head perilously close to the oven. If we needed something from the refrigerator, and invariably there was *some*-thing missing, we all had to get up and move the table in order to open the pink-sprayed refrigerator door. Newspapers were left lying around open to the real estate section, and copies of magazines such as *Better Homes and Gardens* began to spring up like crabgrass all over the house. The subject of "cramped apartments" crept into the conversation, with "spacious estates" hustling in right on its heels. The green suburbs became the new Eden, where your money was invested in property, ownership, status, not just given away to a landlord, and for what? To eat with your elbow in the sink? She wasn't so subtle and he wasn't so dull that the message didn't hit its target.

Our new ten-room house in Short Hills was described by one of the moving men who had delivered chairs and lamps numerous times from the most expensive furniture store in the area. On my way to answer the door, my feet sank deep into the carpet as I passed the bronze copy of the Venus de Milo which stood at the foot of the stairway in the chandeliered front hall, whose walls were papered with hand-flocked curlicues in tempting textures we weren't allowed to touch. Before I came into view, I heard him comment to his partner, "Wait'll you see this place, Joe. It's a fuckin' museum." But it may have been better characterized by my oldest aunt, who pronounced with wide-eyed wonder as she entered the living room, "Just like a movie star's house," beaming at her baby sister, Hannah.

I lasted at this stately pleasure dome for three months. I commuted not only to work but to evening classes at New York University, beginning my Master's degree so I could become a Professor of English Literature (which was not part of the "real" world as doctors were, my mother assured me). The tuition was the straw that broke my back. Surrounded by delivery crates which had just disgorged newly purchased antiques, I was told there wasn't enough money for the next payment. My seventy-dollar salary barely covered the train fare and lunches I consumed to earn it.

"How could you not have the money?" I demanded. "You promised."

"I simply don't have it," she insisted.

"You have enough for all this," I said with a grandiose sweep of my hand, "but not enough for your son's education. Your values are a little distorted, if you ask me."

"Nobody asked you," she snapped.

"All the decent people you copy so much wouldn't come here to visit you anyway," I said. "They know where your money comes from." I knew where to hurt her. I gloated, but only for a moment. I had reduced her to tears. The gloating turned to guilt. She was all too well aware that her movie-star glory was more image than substance. She had been trying to forget.

"Call your father," she said. "Get the money from him."

"What do you need so much education for?" my father the law-school graduate wanted to know. Between them they managed to scrape together the tuition payment.

NYU was a large, impersonal place, where the elevators rose like cattle lifts and a hundred people sat in amphitheater classrooms to hear lectures they might as well have read in books for all the human intercourse there was between teacher and student. We spoke to our teachers in term papers, and I was afraid to write mine. Everyone else in the class seemed so much better equipped than I, older and better read, at least if I could judge by the literary allusions they carefully peppered their statements with.

Afraid to tell my mother, I quit NYU and tried a short bout of psychoanalysis with a doctor who seemed to have more problems than I did, munching cookies behind the couch while I tried to collect my heart enough to pour it out. In his waiting room hung paintings he had done, full of artless demons and distorted monsters that looked worse than my nightmares could ever hope to. I gave him up soon too. For sheer refuge I decided to go to stay with my father. I needed a rest from my life. An hour before my friend Gerry came to pick me up in a small car that easily held all my earthly belongings, I announced simply, "I left school, and I'm leaving here. I'm moving out today."

My mother was obviously stunned and damned if she would say it. I had hoped she would beg me to stay, promise to change our relationship, but her only comment was "All right, Arnold. You've never been happy here. Go." We spent the hour in cold silence until Gerry arrived. My jaw was still clenched when I got to my father's house.

Compared to Short Hills, Clinton Place seemed dowdy. I stayed just long enough to save enough money for an apartment in downtown Newark, only a few blocks from my alma mater. It was even seamier than Clinton Place, but it was the best I could afford, and half of it was all mine. I met my roommate through a friend from school. He was as gay as I was, but we never mentioned the subject to each other. We shared two drab rooms that were somehow large enough for both of us along with our heterosexual closets. We both dated women, and as far as we or our dates were concerned, everyone was straight. I stayed there only a matter of months, but I found time to sneak in an extracurricular crash course in Newark's after-hours gay life.

I learned the art of cruising around Washington Park in the dead of night, in front of the silent doors of Rutgers. The commerce was always between the men who walked and the men who drove, rarely driver to driver parking together on a side street to negotiate, and never walker to walker, face to face. We almost never learned each other's last name, sometimes not even the first. (When we did trade first names, there was a suspiciously huge number of men named John.) This was not to be considered a part of our real lives. It was some sort of dream. If we met the next day, we pretended not to know each other.

When a driver had cruised around the small park enough times to choose his target, he would pull over, leaning conspicuously low in the front seat to watch him pass. I would make snap decisions based on the shape of a fender and what I could imagine of the face in the darkness of the car. Or drivers would sit in parked cars, and I would linger and loiter as obviously as I could, until they gave some sign that I should get in. I moved swiftly, pushed by fear of police cars behind me and pulled ahead by the fear of losing my prize.

I remember going home with drivers only a few times. Many of them were married men, and many were single men who still lived with their parents. Sometimes there would be an empty crib in the corner or an old father asleep down the hall. On a few occasions I also got to sample the quickie hotels of downtown Newark, decorated in the cheery style of the Great Depression, no questions asked. Once or twice I was driven to Branchbrook Park, where we hid in the bushes and got muddy knees. But most of the sex took place in the cars. It wasn't quite like lovers' lane; it was more often parked on a deserted side street, sometimes in front of a respectable one-family house, which might occasion the turning on of porch lights and a great hue and cry demanding a hasty retreat by us. Sometimes the car would even keep moving, as I attempted not to jostle the knee that led to the gas pedal while I wedged my head between steering wheel and crotch, hoping he would have his orgasm while we were safely stopped for a red light, and wondering what would happen if a busload of inquisitive eyes were to pull alongside us.

Some drivers preferred the relative privacy of a closed parking lot, but even that had its dangers. My face nuzzled with happy oblivion in someone's lap in the front seat of a large Lincoln Continental in the shadows deep inside a parking lot closed for the night. My partner was a good catch, attractive enough for me to have promised him "gas money." His cock was firm, his head back, his eyes closed in his own pleasure, when suddenly the peace was disturbed by a bright light shining into the car. Cops!

"We caught two of 'em, Marty, right in the act. Dirty cocksuckers." The voice was matter-of-fact. We pulled ourselves together shamefacedly and got out of the car. They went through our identification, making a big fuss about how much trouble we were in, telling us that our families and employers would be notified, that it was really disgusting how we ruined our own lives, and how nice it would be if we didn't have all this trouble facing us. Then one of them looked me in the eye and said, "You got any money, kid?"

They left me bus fare, taking twenty-seven dollars I could ill afford on my salary. As soon as they had gone, my partner in sin asked, "Do you have enough left to give me the gas money? I ain't queer, just broke." I shook my head, and he drove off in his Continental, disgruntled.

One guy said nothing about "gas money" but waited until I had finished wiping my lips before he pulled out a knife and demanded exactly fifteen dollars, so I should know it was a payment and not a robbery. The distinction was lost on me, but I didn't need to be duped. My own greed could undo me as easily as my defenselessness. I was dumb enough to get into a car with four handsome guys, their bronzed arms and white undershirts evoking fantasies I had enjoyed on the boardwalk of Seaside Heights only a few summers earlier. They drove me to a dead-end street in Harrison, a nearby town, which is desolate by day and closed by night, and they pointed a pistol at me, demanding my wallet and my jewelry, while I calmly pleaded for my school ring and some carfare. I got both, but the ring was stolen a few years later anyway. I was easy prey for everybody. Who was I going to call, the police?

The only time I got to take anyone to my place was when my roommate was out, which was rarely. On one of those few occasions I met the driver of a bread truck, who weakened my knees with his knowing glance. Being in bed was a rare treat. There was no hugging or kissing, but I wasn't accustomed to that anyway, and I was already content enough when he asked, "Do you take it up the ass?"

Why not? I thought, and I answered, "Sure," without hesitation. He rolled me over, anointed himself with some spit, since I wasn't prepared with any more sophisticated lubricant, and he rammed his cock home, eliminating my virginity without a care in the world. I felt like Fay Wray's nightmares about King Kong.

As I mopped up the blood and semen afterward, I vowed never to break the sodomy law again. But not much later I discovered the art of relaxing the sphincter and welcoming men inside me, and I gladly broke that vow as often as I could.

Life in downtown Newark was enough to make me feel genuine relief when my mother made contact and invited me home for Thanksgiving. I thought she might have a birthday celebration for me in mind, but it turned out to be a gathering of her seven sisters and brothers and their assorted mates and children. She had gone all out: as I arrived, two maids were laying shrimp into crystal cups that held green-dyed ice.

"Would you mind eating in the kitchen?" my mother asked sweetly. "There's no room at the dining table because too many children came along."

"Not on your life," I retaliated with instant fury. "Either I eat at the table or I leave."

She had needles in her eyes, but I ate at the table, squeezed into place. I had made my point. From then on if there wasn't affection, there was at least respect, even when we fought.

It took only a few months for her to convince me to move back to Short Hills and to re-enroll at NYU. I quit my job at Channel Five and devoted a year to my Master of Arts degree. This time I tried something new. Instead of letting myself be intimidated by the other students, I tried confiding in them, letting slip when I hadn't done an assignment or felt insulted by a professor's pomposity. And to my amazement they agreed! They felt as ill prepared and as abused as I, but each had been afraid to tell the others, afraid of being the only one. A little honesty felt good. I did well in school. My term papers were as long and pretentious as anyone's, and I even dared to feel a little proud of myself.

I took pleasure from what I read, especially from Walt Whitman, no matter how callously it might be taught. And I took pleasure from the men's rooms at NYU. They were better than the ones at Port Authority. There were no attendants, and in several of the many bathrooms at certain times of day one might chance upon an entire orgy in progress, holding its collective breath only at the sound of approaching footsteps and gladly welcoming each newcomer willing to join. It was a boring wait for everyone—inspecting fingernails and combing hair to shreds—if the newcomer actually had to use the plumbing.

By the end of the school year I had my Master's degree, and just before the beginning of the fall term in 1963, I landed a job at the State University in Cortland, New York. It was a choice between Cortland and North Borneo. (I had applied to the Peace Corps, swept up in the Camelot idealism of the Kennedy administration.) I chose Cortland, figuring it would be exotic enough for my tastes. I knew there wouldn't be much opportunity for a sex life in such a small town. It had no Port Authority, no Washington Park. But I was ready, I thought, to relinquish the life of the body, which was so full of distress, and lead a life of the mind. I envisioned myself with pipe and tweeds, pouring Sunday-afternoon tea for visiting students and pontificating on Milton's commas and Coleridge's meters, neither of which I knew a great deal about.

My mother saw me off in the garage of the house in Short Hills. Once again I had packed all my things into my friend Gerry's car, and he was driving me away from my past. *"Zei gesundt, mein Kind,"* my mother said. "Be well, my child." At our moments of greatest closeness (or when she wanted to keep something secret from my stepfather) she often lapsed into Yiddish, a language made for mothers. I looked at her closely. Here was the single most powerful force in my life. Was I ready to leave her shelter, her control, and assume responsibility for myself, not simply to go to my father's house, but to my own, in another state? I was afraid, but I was twenty-two, and it was time. As I watched her, moisture filled her eyes, and she began to weep. In spite of all the anger and bitterness that had passed between us, in spite of all the sharing that hadn't taken place, the communication we had missed, could we still be sorry to separate? Our grief was real.

Whatever her demands, whatever my failures to meet them, there was a bond between us that would always hold us close. We embraced like two exhausted boxers in the ring. If there were wrath and rejection, there were attachment and need in equal measure. If we couldn't avoid fury, we couldn't avoid love either. There was love. One of those things you learn to appreciate only when you say good-bye. *There was love.* I sniffled away my hurt for the first hundred miles on the road to my new life.

Cortland, New York, was not my Emerald City. It sat rather like a wart composed of minor industries and tired houses squat in the middle of the gently rolling farm hills in the center of the state. It had been the home base of the squalid murder of a pregnant factory worker by a revivalist's son who wanted to marry a rich girl, a deed which Theodore Dreiser embalmed as *An American Tragedy. A Place in the Sun,* Hollywood called it, with Elizabeth Taylor, who I doubt would have made it there for the year and a half that I did.

I lived in a converted one-family house that contained one other apartment, a lawyer's office, and a beauty parlor. The beauty parlor gave way to an apartment full of students, and I hung around with them through homework and hair dyeing, surprise pregnancy and sudden marriage. Upstairs I occupied what had once been two rooms, now connected: one a living room, the other divided partway between a narrow kitchen and a windowless tunnel of a bedroom. It was furnished something like an impoverished dentist's office with the best I could afford: a foam-rubber couch whose cushions got strangled in the frame when anyone sat down (but which did open up into an uncomfortable bed), a vinyl Danish-modern chair, a bridge table, a dresser with pseudo-Oriental handles, and, for a while, even a rented piano.

I had sex with three men the whole time I was there. They were exhausted salesmen I picked up during my middle-of-the-night forays along the four silent blocks of shopwindows that constituted Main Street. They were mainly looking for a place to fall asleep. The rest of my gay life consisted of masturbating over daringly purchased magazines with pictures of men in bathing suits and posing straps, which I hid at the bottom of a suitcase in back of my closet, and combing my hair with inordinately fastidious slowness in the mirror that reflected the open door of the men's locker room at school, where an occasional flash of flesh might appear. I didn't dare to think of touching a student. That might infect them with my secret leprosy.

If there was any problem in Cortland's reception of me, it wasn't for being gay: it was for being Jewish! Anti-Semitism, in polite form, was alive and well in Cortland. My landlord was a decent person, but it was not considered fashionable to rent to Jews, at least not by the old guard, the ones who minded so much when someone would go to the library to fetch the yellowed accounts of the town's celebrated murder case from the newspaper files. Such were the chairladies of the town's welcoming committee.

First came Mrs. Edgeworth. Still moving in, I pulled up a carton and offered her coffee and a plate of Oreo cookies. She was the bank president's wife, I learned immediately. After a thorough conversational probe of my history and credentials she informed me, "Personally, I tend to mingle with the high types."

"High types?" I asked, eyebrows up.

"I do play bridge with some of the school administrators."

"How nice," I offered.

"There are people you'd like to know here too," she said condescendingly. "I'll be sure to send my husband over with a list of names for you."

She left me with a book of coupons for the local stores, evidently not assembled for single men, since it included discounts at the beauty parlor and the dess shop.

Mrs. Biedermeier rang the bell while Mrs. Edgeworth was still there. "Oh! Claudia!" she said with ice. "I had no idea *you* were here."

"Sorry, Martha," dripped Mrs. Edgeworth. "I was just leaving."

I felt caught between the leaders of competing covens.

"Kantrowitz," Mrs. Biedermeier murmured unctuously. "Is that a . . . *Hebrew* name?"

"If you mean, 'Am I Jewish?' " I said, "yes."

"Oh. Well, ah, they're nice too," she said. She also gave me a coupon book.

Mrs. Edgeworth's husband showed up that afternoon with the list of names she had promised. I was impressed at having a bank president for a messenger until he gave me some brochures and told me the advantages of opening an account at his bank rather than the larger one across the street. (I wondered where the high types kept their money.) As soon as he'd gone, I checked the list. Every name on it was Jewish. A list of gay people would have helped more.

When the Jewish New Year came, in early September, I made my way to the one-family house whose living room was the local synagogue. There were some thirty people in the congregation, and strange though it seemed to be in a *schul* after all those years, even without being able to follow the service in Hebrew, somehow I needed the comfort of knowing I was not alone. Some of my students were there too. They looked at me knowingly, with a special sense of kinship when they saw me in school after that.

The first class I taught was a trauma I had dreaded for years, like my Bar Mitzvah. I had been assured that the hour would be taken up with the filling out of forms and the passing out of papers and the listing of books. All of that took a total of ten minutes, and there were thirty expectant faces waiting in front of me to hear the story of American literature. The morning I had prepared a few hasty comments on the Puritans for use on the second day, and I turned to them and began to read. When I looked up, I saw that they were taking notes! Whatever little I knew was more than they did. I finished the hour with ease, bopped into my next class, and began with a few jokes. Scholarship had been like Judaism and heterosexuality. I had felt like a fraud at all of them. I was only a few years older than my students, and I hid behind the pomposity that was expected of me when I taught them. From behind the role of Instructor of English, I could reach them. Most of them were majoring in physical education and weren't too thrilled by English, but when I made Joe Zampi's eyes light up with interest and he told me proudly that for the first time he was understanding poetry, I knew I wasn't an Educated Nothing. I could teach! I was an Educated Something.

Alice Birch thought so when I met her on a stone bench in front of the Administration Building. She was also a new English teacher, not as happy with her results as I was with mine, she told me quietly. She thought, she later confided in me, that I looked like a "Formidable Young Scholar" type, and I thought the same of her. I didn't think she was pretty. Her owlish, horn-rimmed glasses set on her square face made her look academic. Her untended hair, a lovely shade of

real blond, hung limply alongside her cheeks. But soon
I learned she was beautiful.

We became fast friends, visiting each other, shopping
at the supermarket together, eating dinner out. Together
we met the single teachers who drank at the English
Department's weekly "Happy Hour" by the light of
pink bulbs silhouetting plastic flower arrangements at
the Cortland Hotel's bar. All of us had a sort of earnest-
ness and a lot of free time. We played charades, made
dinner for each other, followed by entertainment such
as slides of somebody's trip to Turkey, and we drank.
We went to the Family Bargain Center, Alice and I
snickering with our big-city sophistication at the back-
wardness of the local fashion. Sometimes we would
drive to Ithaca to see a foreign movie at Cornell. And
then we drank. Or the men would go to Syracuse to
see a stripper at André's Tic-Toc Club or a belly dancer
at the Hajii Baba and be embarrassed, each of us for
his own reasons, and drink. Sometimes the young married teachers would have some of us to dinner. Those
invitations were usually sincere. Sometimes the older
members of the department would invite us. Those
invitations were usually political. In either case, we
drank. Mostly we hung out with each other. After growing up in a house where the lone bottle of Scotch was
perpetually half full, waiting for genuine medicinal
purposes, I learned to tolerate the alcohol that lubri-
cated Cortland's social life quite well, without over-
doing it.

I was too busy discovering Alice, reading Betty
Friedan, and growing excited with her about the liberation of women, going for long rides, just talking. We
lived through John Kennedy's assassination together,
sharing our sudden grief that the administration they
called Camelot was as easily shattered as a delicate
bisque lamp and could be inherited by Lyndon Baines

Johnson's crassness. Our framework seemed loose, rattling in the night wind, and we wondered, along with everyone, whether our foundations were secure. Occupied with these thoughts, the first year of teaching went by. At the end of it Alice wasn't rehired.

I taught summer school, enjoying the melancholy summer afternoons on hillsides just outside town. But as autumn set in and I found myself alone, I sank into a deepening gloom that eventually became constant. I stopped marking freshman papers, stalling the students with promises, preparing as little as I could to get through class, spending long hours playing sad songs on the rented piano, lying on my bed, scrutinizing the ceiling. I missed Alice. She was traveling across the country, sending me postcards from places where cactus grew, and each time I heard from her, I was more anxious to see her again.

She came to visit in December, soon after she had returned from California, but she didn't lift my gloom. She slept on the foam-rubber couch in my living room, and she acted very inviting, but I was frightened. She made the mistake of answering the doorbell in her bathrobe twice. Once it was a student of mine selling Christmas cookies and beating a red-faced retreat. The other time it was two of the older women in the English Department. "It's all right," they chirped cheerily over their shoulders as they rushed right back down the stairs. "We understand *perfectly!*" But there had been nothing to understand. I got as far as into bed with her, but I couldn't do anything.

At the department's Christmas party a psychology teacher whose husband taught English took me aside. "I'm sorry to see you so depressed lately," she said. "I know what you are, and I think you're worth ten of him any day." She pointed to another young English teacher whose wife had just had a baby.

I looked at her aghast. "How can you tell what I am?"

"I've had plenty of experience with homosexuals," she said. It was the first time anyone had applied the label to me. I was horrified. I was becoming visible.

By the end of the week it was evident to Alice that something was the matter. It was the night before we were going to drive home for Christmas vacation. I had to tell her, but I couldn't. I had never told anyone about myself. She could see I was growing distraught. Finally I took the plunge.

"There's something I have to tell you," I mumbled after a long, morose silence.

"What?" she asked. She waited.

I couldn't answer. There was no way I could bring that shame from my most guarded depths to the surface. I knew I had to, and I struggled, but I couldn't. I paced from room to room.

"What's wrong? Surely there's nothing so terrible that you can't tell me," she comforted.

"I can't," I said. "I can't."

It went on for well over two hours. Finally, exhausted, I lay on my bed, tossing my head from side to side, wracked with the battle between the need to explain and declaring myself unhuman. Alice came into the room.

"Tell me," she said softly. "What could make you torture yourself like this?"

"I . . . I can't." I was weeping.

"Please," she said.

"Can't you guess?" I tried getting her to say the words.

"What is it?"

"I . . . I'm . . . a homosexual." It was out.

She sat quietly. I could hear her begin to weep. I couldn't look at her. "But I love you," she whispered.

"And I love you," I said.

The drive home was nearly silent. I remember nothing about the vacation except a depression so deep I could barely stir or speak. At the end of it I collected myself into a colleague's car and let myself be taken back.

The first day of classes was too much to face. I stayed home, not even calling in sick, convinced I had already ruined my career. I only wanted to be asleep, unconscious of the world.

Tension had upset my stomach, and the doctor had prescribed tranquilizers. I knew what I had to do. I took my physique magazines from the bottom of their suitcase in the back of the closet and buried them in someone else's garbage can. I went calmly to the medicine chest, and I patiently and deliberately swallowed twenty-four of the pills, one for each year of my life.

I awoke to the sound of the phone an hour later, one of the teachers wanting to know if I wanted to have dinner out. "No thanks, I can't," I said, almost wanting to explain, "I'm committing suicide."

I ran into the bathroom and heaved my guts up. I was exhausted beyond tiredness, defeated beyond feeling, operating mechanically to do what I knew had to be done. I wrote and rewrote a suicide note, so whoever found me wouldn't think I had been murdered. The eighth and final version read: "I am destroying myself because I find it impossible to continue living. Please contact Sydney Kantrowitz at the following address. . . ."

I took a fresh razor blade from the pack and stood at the sink, which I filled with hot water. I cut at my left wrist and found that "slash" is the wrong word. I had to saw. The blood began to flow profusely, coloring the water with a horror I could barely stand to see.

I wrapped my arm in a loose towel and went to lie down, to sleep.

Half an hour later I woke up, realizing I hadn't succeeded in cutting the artery. I made my way back to the bathroom, struggling with my rapidly waning courage, and unwrapped my arm. The bleeding had stopped, and the wound gaped at me like an obscene red eye. Somewhere I found the strength to put the razor blade back into it and saw still deeper. Again the blood flowed, and again I went to lie down. This time I didn't fall asleep. I wanted so much to sleep.

I went back again, and I cut my right wrist at a different spot. Again I bled. Again I lay down to die.

This time when I awoke, I knew I had done as much as I could and had failed. I called Alice at her parents' house in the Bronx. She told me to stay put and called one of the other teachers to help me. I called my father. "Dad, I need help. I just tried to kill myself. I cut my wrists."

"Where are you?"

"In Cortland, at my apartment."

"What did you do?"

"I cut my wrists. They're still bleeding, but I guess I didn't cut the right places."

"I want you to get on a bus and come home."

Bus? I thought. "Sure, Dad. Thanks."

Then came a confusion of phone calls, from Alice, from the teacher who was on his way over, finally from my mother.

"My son," she said with formal compassion, "what did you do to yourself? Your father called me."

"I cut my wrists. I wanted to die."

"Don't go to the hospital. They have to report it to the police. Go to a private doctor. Do you want me to come up there?"

"Very much," I answered. I needed to be someone's

child at that moment. While I was doctored and put up at my collegue's house, my mother and Frank and Ira drove through the night and arrived at dawn. When we got back to my apartment, she took me alone into my bedroom.

"Arnold," she said, "tell me. There must be a reason. What made you do this terrible thing?"

"I'm a homosexual," I said matter-of-factly, too tired to explain any further.

Tears filled her eyes. But she rejoined immediately, "This is no reason to die. Everybody has something to live with."

Then she took me into the kitchen and stood me near the stove, reaching for a box of coarse kosher salt I kept on the countertop. She turned on a flame and took a handful of salt and sprinkled some on my head and then sprinkled some in the fire, repeating the sequence two more times. Then she spit three times over her left shoulder and began to mumble in Yiddish, turning from a bleached American matron into a Russian Jewish peasant right in front of me.

"What are you doing?" I asked with widened eyes.

"Shh," she said. "I'm saying a curse against the Evil Eye."

I returned from New Jersey two weeks later with freshly unbandaged wrists. Alice drove me back to help me finish the semester, which was the most I could enlist to do before going home again to collapse. I had left with only a hasty phone call to tell the secretary of the English Department that I was ill and was going to visit my family to recuperate. Somehow a great mystery had developed around my sudden disappearance. The few people who knew anything about it remained silent on my behalf, and I was greeted with rumors about my being a crazed dope addict at large in

Chicago or the fleeing father of a sophomore's pregnancy. My description had even been broadcast on local radio as a missing person! With a few embarrassed excuses about a "nervous collapse" and long sweater sleeves to hide my new scars, I halfheartedly marked the semester's papers that lay waiting in a pile. Alice pitched in, and the whole department helped to cover my classes. I made my only public appearance at the final exams. I sold some of my furniture to the landlord and packed the rest into a U-Haul trailer and let Alice drive me along the perilously icy winter road back to where I had come from. It wasn't quite Auntie Em's farm in Kansas. So that I could be close to a psychoanalyst in New York, I had agreed to live with my father in Newark.

4

I SPENT THE FIRST SIX MONTHS OF 1965 IN THE DARK-ened living room of the house on Clinton Place, with sunglasses on and a pillow over my face. I had been a fetus there before. It was the same apartment my parents had lived in when I was born. I slept in the living room on a convertible couch. My father slept in what had once been his bridegroom's room and most lately his sister's room until her husband had died. He surrounded himself with a bizarre collection of furnishings: a dresser that dated back to when he had been married, a gym locker from a company he had worked in that had gone out of business, two broken television sets, one atop the other, and a collection of empty hair-tonic bottles and used razor blades and ball-point pens that had run out of ink. He had some difficulty throwing things away.

He tried to offer me comfort, not knowing what was wrong or whether he was in some way responsible. "I love you," he said for the one and only time in my life. He said it with the clumsiness that men of his genera-tion feel when discussing emotions. I felt awkward but responded in kind, yet I didn't discuss my homosexuality. I was afraid that he wouldn't understand it, that he would be angry with me, so I didn't share much of myself. I muffled reality with the pillow I buried my face in. When summer came, my father slept with an air conditioner on, his locked door blocking the cross ventilation in the rest of the apartment.

In spite of the heat, Aunt Ruth, my father's sister, slept with her door shut as well, out of modesty. But in the kitchen we were bosom buddies. The kitchen clock always said eight-twenty. The room had once been painted a happy yellow, but too many years without renewal had made it stop trying. The table was tucked into a niche where only two people could squeeze. It had an easily tipped-over table lamp that did little to aid my reading of escape fiction or my aunt's sewing buttons or manicuring or working the Sunday *Times* crossword puzzle—we got two copies—or my once-a-week breakfasts with my father when he had finished delivering the Saturday-night bagels and had brought home the freshest smoked fish in the city. Aunt Ruth and I would complain to each other across the table over a thousand cups of coffee and twice as many cigarettes. When we had worked up a good melancholy mood, we went to the piano, whose bench touched the foot of the Hide-a-Bed I slept on, and we traded sad melodies: Yiddish songs and show tunes and torch songs from the movies. Her Chopin cheered us both as we sat beneath her reproduction of a Napoleonic drawing-room scene, three gowned young ladies at the traditional musical instruments. The stuffing was coming out of a rip in the couch. My Danish-modern chair was squeezed into a corner. My dresser stood beneath her shadow box and its knicknacks and figurines. Most of the time while my father and my aunt were at work,

I sat in that room and tried to teach myself the wistful slow movement from Beethoven's "Pathétique Sonata."

Down on the first floor lived my father's bachelor brother, Henry, nursing Grandpa Simon, who was dying of bone cancer.

Grandpa came from another world and time. His hair and his tidy moustache were bright white in his early eighties. He had come here at the turn of the century to avoid fifteen years in the Tsar's army. His family, save for a nephew in Argentina—a doctor— and a cousin in Israel, had been wiped out by the Nazis. He showed me photographs of his bearded father and his stern-eyed mother. He had built his own surroundings, including the house we lived in, where he wanted to die. He had built it for Grandma Sarah, who had married him while he was still a carpenter, raised his four children, seen him through his career in real estate, and died nine years before. The girl in their wedding picture was slim and softly beautiful. The Grandma I had known was fat and jolly and made me French toast and cocoa for breakfast when I stayed over with my mother's salt in my pocket warding off the Evil Eye. Appearances mattered. Grandpa had never appeared in public without a tie and jacket, not even in the years when, wearing his household Bermuda shorts, he could be taken for a ride to have ice cream in suburban South Orange. In spite of the shorts on everyone in sight, he refused to get out of the car. Now he only sat in a rocking chair or lay in bed. He read *The Jewish Daily Forward*. He was kosher, laughing with silent pretense when I remarked that there was butter on the table while he was eating meat. He had at long last discovered margarine. He observed the holidays, but he didn't think too much of rabbis, and he never made a regular habit of going to temple. He was modern enough to assert that maybe I didn't have to marry a rich Jewish girl. Maybe just a nice girl would suffice. I didn't even think of asking what he thought about a nice boy. But I would have. Grandpa was stern with his own children but more indulgent with me. He had a stubborn allegiance to decorum that inspired respect and loyalty in all of us, however aloof he seemed. It was to Grandpa Simon that I had written when I first got to Cortland, about my admiration for his courage in starting a new life in a new place. He wanted to frame the letter, Uncle Henry told me.

If two more idiosyncratic people than Uncle Henry and Grandpa Simon ever played odd couple, I'd like to see their house. Maybe the most characteristic note of the first-floor apartment in the house on Clinton Place was the garbage chair in the kitchen. In the large space where Grandma Sarah used to serve salami and eggs, a *Feinkuchen,* to be eaten with a pinch of course salt right from the crusty black frying pan set on a plate, there remained three out of the original four chairs around the blue Formica-topped table. The fourth stood permanently alone, the only object against the middle of its wide expanse of scrubbed tile wall, and supported a bag of garbage. Grandma would never have condoned this, not in the same kitchen with her made-in-Japan knickknacks still on the rounded shelves built into the corner, even if her organdy curtains had given way to one white and one green window shade. Not only was the garbage chair aesthetically puzzling, but it was permanently unavailable for use. It was doubtless a contribution of Uncle Henry's penchant for cleanliness.

I have never seen anyone else wash the skin of a banana before peeling it. All jars and cans were thoroughly scrubbed before opening, germs being even more insidious than drafts. Aunt Ruth once surprised him at the kitchen sink using a soapy Brillo pad to scrub a lemon before inserting it into his tea. The most difficult sanitary problem for Uncle Henry was his brother my Uncle Arthur, the suburbanite. Uncle Arthur was given to little habits like eating from a spoon and then dipping it into the mayonnaise jar. Henry would quietly cap the jar and throw the whole thing in the garbage, which was never an unnoticed gesture because of the prominent position of the garbage bag on its chair. Afterward there would be a rubber-gloved washing of dishes, fraught with soapy bubbles and great clouds of steam.

In spite of all our personal foibles, we could stir much laughter and song. Ruth would always have a waltz ready. Henry played the violin, usually classical music; and Arthur played progressive jazz on the piano. But when they were together, they would join in Yiddish classics like "Hora Staccata" and "Roumania," especially at the Passover seders which were our favorite occasions. Sometimes we would begin giggling at a long table full of uncles, aunts, and cousins, and the laughter would sweep infectiously back and forth from one end of the table to the other and back again until all of us were drying our streaming eyes with our napkins and wondering what had been so funny in the first place. While Grandpa Simon presided over such occasions, which took place in Arthur's house where there was more room for cooking, he would remind us of the solemnity of the occasion. But he could never erase the twinkle from Arthur's eye.

Uncle Arthur dreamed of being on the stage, and the amateur productions he starred in only whetted his appetite for more. He envied his oldest son's daring in forming a rock band at the same time that he yelled at him for growing his hair so long and fought with the high-school principal to let it stay that way. He would sit at the kitchen table on Clinton Place and enthrall us all with tales of what he would do when his star finally rose. It was tempting to believe him until we looked away from his eyes and surveyed the squalid tidiness that surrounded the house, whose life was insulated from its environs by a thick bank of memory. Its world of chicken fat and Grandma's yellowing antimacassars ended at the front door, where Newark had become a tortured black ghetto.

Gone were the transporting delights of Cohen's knishes and hot rolls from Silver's bakery, with its fresh rye bread whose paper label could never be removed without taking a chunk of the delicious crust along with it. The lox and bagels were gone, as was the candy store presided over by a ubiquitous mother who worried that I might spoil my dinner if I ordered an afternoon malted milk, composed of a big foamy glassful and a large metal container waiting beside it, half-filled with still more. On their sites stood soul-food grocery stores, shoeshine parlors, and "The La Vogue Beauty Shoppe," its windows adorned with portaits of black women with painstakingly straightened hair, eventually giving way to self-conscious Afros. Suddenly, it seemed without anyone having noticed, there was hatred in the eyes we encountered in the streets, hatred for the political entity called "Whitey," and being Jewish didn't help. We were the last white Jews in the neighborhood. I didn't go out too often to face the world: a trip to the grocery, a visit to a friend, an occasional day full of two double-feature movie programs; and once a week I traveled to New York to be psychoanalyzed.

The first time I went to see the analyst, I didn't know what to expect. My mother had been referred to him by another doctor, and we knew nothing about all this, except that I'd probably have to shop through several doctors. He turned out to be a gentle, unprepossessing man, tidily attired in tweeds. His office bookcases held an accumulated assortment of personal mementos, colorful against the quiet gray walls. I sat in a chair facing him, and I told him my story: my memories of my family, my sexual experiences, my feelings. He listened with patience, occasionally interrupting with a carefully chosen question that sent my monologue in intriguing directions. He accepted the most intimate details of my life with equanimity. I wanted to be able to trust him, but instead I challenged him.

"I feel like such a weak person. I can't be cured," I said.

"You're a strong person if you got this far," he assured me.

"I write poetry," I said. "I hope this treatment won't 'cure' me of that."

"Neurosis gets in the way of your poetry. It doesn't help it."

"But I do want to be cured of my homosexuality." I switched my tack. "Do you think we can manage that?"

"Maybe I can help you to find out who you are and how to be that person. If you really are interested in sleeping with a woman, maybe I can help you to express that feeling in physical terms. If you are really interested, that is."

I had noticed something gentle about him, and perhaps he was a little too well-groomed. Maybe there was an Achilles' heel. "I've told you I'm a homosexual," I said, working to keep the accusation out of my voice, "and I have to be honest with you. I can't avoid the feeling that you're one too!"

He looked at me hard. Then he answered, "Our time is up. Next week at this time is free. Would you like an appointment?"

"Yes," I said.

For a whole week I wondered if I had managed to find the only gay analyst in the world. He hadn't denied it. What if he is? I wondered to myself. Can I trust him? If he's weak enough to be like I am, how can he help me to unearth my manhood, to make it with Alice?

By the time I returned for the second session, I wasn't at all sure I wanted to be there. It might do me more harm than good. But he hadn't said anything. Maybe it was all in my mind.

Soon after we began, he said, looking me right in the eye calmly, "At the end of our last talk, you told me you thought I might be homosexual. I don't usually discuss my personal life with my patients, but I'm going to be honest with you. I am. I've lived with the same man for almost twenty-five years now, and we still love each other. The only times we're 'unfaithful' to each other is when we go on vacation. He does social work, and we're both very busy so there's never enough time for us, but we spend all our free time together. No one knows for sure that we're lovers, but everyone who knows us—our friends, our families, our professional colleagues—all treat us as a couple. We're invited to dinner together out at my mother's, or here at friends' houses. Or the two of us will join our married friends at the theater. We just don't discuss what we do in bed."

I admired his candor. I admired what seemed to me an unparalleled open lifestyle. But it wasn't what he said that convinced me so much as the quiet firmness in his tone. There was something fatherly about him, something competent belied by his gentle demeanor.

"Maybe this will affect your decision about continuing to come here," he continued, "but it seems only fair that you should know before you make up your mind. I have a special sympathy for the problem you're facing, but I'm not interested in proselytizing you into being homosexual, only in helping you to be yourself, whoever that turns out to be. Do you think you want to continue treatment?"

"Yes," I said.

I was soon worried about Alice. We were meeting after my appointments with the analyst, going for window-shopping walks and cups of coffee in small restaurants and dinner at her house. On the way home I would stop at the Port Authority terminal men's room and cruise Washington Park back in Newark. I found myself seducing men into mastering me, enjoying whatever fantasies of degradation I could get them to act out with me. I didn't know what to tell Alice about our future, but I had to tell her something.

"Should I tell Alice there's a chance?" I asked the doctor.

"There's no telling who you'll turn out to be," he reminded me. "If Alice wants to wait to see what happens, that's her decision. Even if you turn to women, there's no guarantee that you'll want her. All you owe her is sincerity. The rest is up to her."

"How long will it take to know?" I asked.

"There's no way to tell," he said.

I told Alice everything he had said, and I finished with, "It's your decision."

She asked, "How long will it take to know?"

"There's no way to tell."

"I'll wait," she said softly. She waited five years.

Sometime during that first year, I arrived at the doctor's office feeling agitated. I can't remember what we talked about because a feeling of excitement kept mounting inside me. Near the end of the session I told the doctor, "Fifty minutes isn't enough to let this out. I feel as if a great, golden truth is about to burst inside my chest." But fifty minutes was all we had. I left, unfinished, to meet Alice.

That afteroon was one of the few moments that

could merit all her years of patience and warmth and understanding. I told her how I felt, and she stayed with me through it. It was bliss. Again I belonged to everything as I had belonged to it when I had looked out of the bus window at the dreariness of the northern New Jersey landscape a few years earlier and seen it transfigured. I had experienced that feeling of unity several times since, but only for brief moments. This time it lasted for hours into the evening. The world seemed all beautiful. I felt beautiful. Everything was melting together, losing its solid definition, and I wanted to inscribe my name in the liquid sidewalk with the tip of my shoe. I wrote pages of glowing poetry, with images of swallowing sunlight and embracing the earth. There was something in it beyond words, something I didn't simply believe in, but *knew* with utter certainty to be true, something that glowed for days in the wake of feeling it.

Of course, I was afraid I was going mad, but I was too sure the feeling I had had was positive to believe that. At my next appointment with the doctor I poured out the story breathlessly, showing him what I had written, offering to bring in Alice as a witness.

"You had a *satori*," he said.

"What's a *satori*?"

"It's a Zen term. It means 'spontaneous enlightenment,' a sudden flash of seeing the unity of things." He went to the bookcase and selected a volume of Alan Watts's Oriental philosophy, offering it to me. I felt a great kinship with what I read. It spoke of the meanings of life and death at a time when they loomed large at home.

I watched as Grandpa Simon's life began to ebb. He was spending more time in the hospital than at home, in ever increasing pain. I spent my afternoons visiting him, helping with his lunch, and keeping him company.

Once, when he gave me his hand to hold, I noticed it was streaked with brown, with his own shit, where he had attempted to scratch away at the excruciating pain that had reached his bowels. I took his hand and held it, and I tried to tell him that I loved him. I was awkward. He flashed me a hard stare to ask who I was through his morphine haze, looking at me with startled recognition, with a flash of his old dignity, and he said, "I know," and held my hand tight. I went home and practiced Beethoven's "Pathétique."

One night when Aunt Ruth came home from work and we sat over coffee and cigarettes, I mused, "If I were dying, I think I'd like to know, so I could finish my thoughts and organize myself to go, and say goodbye to the people I love."

She flew into hysteria. "It isn't bad enough my father's dying? Now you want to tell him and make it worse for him? How could you be so cruel?"

"I didn't mean Grandpa," I said. "I was really thinking about an abstract idea."

It took some time to calm her down. She wasn't used to venting her feelings. Of course, I never told Grandpa the truth. But he probably knew anyway. He was nobody's fool. He lay silent, keeping his dying to himself. It was a matter of appearances. I turned my attention to living, and to the rest of my family.

Appearances were important for my brother too. Ira had been raised amid the opulent glamour of Short Hills. His memories of Newark were dim. But the glamour had bedazzled him into forgetting to do his homework, and in order to improve his grades he was planted in a Pennsylvania military academy. My mother and Frank and I visited him there.

I had already developed quite a distaste for military regimentation. I had been so anxious to avoid military service that I had let the doctor write my draft board a letter telling them how my homosexuality allowed me to function only marginally. I didn't care about the records. It was worth anything to avoid two years of confinement with a barracks full of attractive young men and a rulebook full of "No." The army's fear of love worked in my favor. The draft board had sent a 4-F almost by return mail. They didn't even call me in for a physical.

My brother greeted us in his uniform, immaculate down to his white gloves, his back erect as if he wore a whalebone corset. I scandalized him by scurrying toward him with my arms folded across my chest for warmth in the late-spring chill.

"Don't walk like that," he cautioned as I shook his hand. "It isn't manly." He was learning his lessons well.

We had time to talk alone for a few minutes, and he confided in me his fears about living up to a code that was so pervasively demanding. He had doubts about whether he could sustain a family, profit at a job, survive the dehumanization he knew he was undergoing. I offered him what reassurance I could from the scant resources I had begun to muster. Then we all went to dinner and a James Bond movie.

When I got into the back seat of Frank's big green Cadillac for the ride home, I decided to mention his confidence to my mother, who had been pleased with the "improvement" she had seen in Ira's conduct.

"Ira told me he's not very happy here," I said. "He sounds like he's really scared about living up to expectations. He sounds insecure. I know what that feels like." I was speaking as a brother and a son. She heard only the voice of a homosexual, and she burst into a rage that lasted the entire three-hour drive home.

"What do you mean, you 'know what that feels like'?" she demanded. "Are you saying Ira's like you? Are you blaming me for your problem?"

"I'm just trying to help him understand himself. We come from the same background, but I don't think he's very much like me at all."

Somehow the subject changed to my failures as a son, a man, a person. A tirade of accusation came pouring down on my head, from my earliest ingratitudes to my present "condition," which is what she called my sex life in front of Frank, who drove silently. "You'd better give up this nonsense before it's too late to get married," she said to me as if Frank weren't there. "You're fat and you wear glasses, and soon you'll be bald and no one will want you." I accepted her judgment behind tightened lips, but she went on and on, airing all her grievances, while I sank into my own thoughts. I emerged to hear, "And I struggled to buy a piano just for you. . . ."

"For me?" I gasped. "For me? You're the one who always wanted to play! You bought that piano for yourself! Buying lessons for your son was for your own glory. I hated practicing that piano!"

"Everything I ever did was for my children!" She raised her voice higher. "Now I get nothing but blame for everything. I gave you all I could. I gave you *too* much! I was *too* good!"

"Looks to me like you managed a few fringe benefits out of all that sacrifice: a mink coat, an eleven-carat diamond ring, a Cadillac!"

"I did it for you," she yelled, "to give you an education, a chance in life, and look at you! I was divorced with two children. I could have made it on my own, but I worked for my children." She was screaming. "Why do you think I fuck for Frank?"

Frank managed not to lose control of the wheel. I could see in the rapid glances he divided between the road and her beside him that it had really stung. "Shut up," he barked.

"I didn't mean. . . ." She sounded frightened.

In the back seat I dreamed of murder.

But my visits to the doctor's office helped to uncork my rage and my confusion safely, enough to let me function by summer. A rest of many months had restored at least some of the energy I had discharged in my suicide attempt. I wanted to escape the stifling living room on Clinton Place. I interviewed for teaching jobs, and with a little help from a friend and all the nervously perspiring boldness I could employ, I ended up at Staten Island Community College with two part-time jobs: two courses in the afternoon and two in the evening session. Every course I had was freshman composition, which meant I was marking papers at all times, especially on the ferries, trains, and buses on which I commuted, stopping in their late-night terminals to join the assortment of men who went through the men's room door if there was enough time before the next train or bus that took me all the way to Newark, where I slept and marked more papers. I wore business suits with neckties left over from my year at Channel Five and tweeds left over from Cortland. I was the liberal iconoclast in the classroom, propagating peace and brotherhood and the proper placement of commas for the uninterested offspring of the working class of Brooklyn and Staten Island. I played Instructor of English, and they played Student, with a few exceptions, the ones who seemed to understand what I was trying to say. They became my friends. I still hear from some of them.

Most of my students, however, were appalled at my refusal to endorse their patriotic politics. In one class I blithely compared the United States and the Soviet Union as impersonal bureaucracies, both of which preferred technological values to human ones. But I had forgotten that it was still the McCarthy Era on Staten

Island. I arrived for the next class meeting to find myself labeled a Communist on the blackboard, suspended from which was Old Glory, poised like a guillotine blade just above my chair. As I entered, the entire class rose to recite the Pledge of Allegiance, insisting menacingly that I join them. Then we discussed a short story that dealt with group pressure on the individual, the Instructor emphasizing the point that one mustn't mistake symbols—like flags—for the realities they represent, and I dragged myself home to Newark.

On a January morning in 1966, while I was preparing to go to school, Grandpa Simon died. I felt as if my own father were gone when we buried him next to Grandma Sarah the following day. The family came back to the house on Clinton Place to begin the mourning week of sitting *shiva,* all of us washing our hands in a bucket of water that waited on the front porch, according to custom. As we gathered around a long table piled with herring and hard-boiled eggs and rolls, it looked almost like a Passover seder, except that Grandpa was missing from the head of the table. And then, strangely, it began to sound like a seder, like the old days, with waves of laughter filling the room. No one knew where it had started. Everyone in the room had loved Grandpa Simon personally. There was no one who was glad to see him die. But we were too embarrassed to cry, and our emotions needed to come out in some way or other. The laughter swept through the whole house uncontrollably, all of us hysterical with it, each of us abashed at our mirth lest the neighbors might wonder.

Alice traveled all the way from the Bronx to pay a condolence call during the week. As I introduced her to the family, I noticed a distinct chill, in spite of all the help she had been to me, which they knew full well. I wondered at the lack of enthusiasm, which was barely covered by belated offerings of politeness. Hadn't I brought home a real live woman? Weren't they glad to see her? I looked at her pale blond hair. I had forgotten that Alice wasn't Jewish, that she was the stranger in our midst, but no one else had. That was Alice's last visit to Newark. I didn't want to expose her to the premarital interrogations that had to be expected by any woman who traveled from the Bronx to Newark to visit a single man.

Marriage was on everyone's mind but mine. One by one my friends were getting married. I served as Gerry's best man that spring, glad to repay him for the loan of his parents years before to hear my childhood sorrows, and glad to repay him for the times he had packed his car with my belongings and driven me away from my mother's house in Short Hills. It was a strange ceremony to me. I felt like a fraud again. It had nothing to do with my beliefs, and as I surveyed the crowd who stood beneath the wedding canopy—the bride and groom, the best man and maid of honor, the parents of the newly married couple—I realized that few people there believed in the ancient strictures any more than I. The rest were there out of deference to tradition. When Gerry crushed the symbolic wineglass beneath his foot, we all cried *"Mazeltov!"* together. But rather than tying me closer to my heritage, it reminded me that I was different. I belonged somewhere else.

5

I HARDLY NOTICED THE ROW OF CURIOUS SHOPWIN-
dows on Christopher Street as I passed on my way to
answer an ad for an apartment a block away: "2½ rms,
$150, a/c, see supt, 350 Bleecker St." The building
looked nothing like the charming Greenwich Village
brownstone I had imagined in my daydreams. It was
creativity I was after, someplace with a soul that hadn't
been vanquished like Newark's. But after a month of
footsore hunting, I no longer expected to find any bargains. I just wanted to be in New York. I just wanted
a home.

"2½ rms" turned out to be an L-shaped studio with
a standup kitchen on the fourth floor of a plastic apartment house with a surly superintendent and a static
view of a brick courtyard. I stood in one corner and
looked around, trying to figure out which part of the L
was the "½," weary of being misled by real estate ads.
The summer of 1966 was hot. The air conditioner
worked. My feet hurt. I decided to take it.

I moved in on Labor Day weekend, which I spent
unpacking books and rewashing dishes. The fall semes-

ter was about to begin, and I wanted to be settled in
before I faced my first full-time year at Staten Island
Community College. It wasn't until well after midnight
on Monday that I finally had a chance to go out for a
walk to explore my new neighborhood, window-shopping and marveling at how heavy the pedestrian traffic
was for that hour on a weeknight. Then, as I walked
down Christopher Street, everything changed all at
once, as if by some miracle I was glimpsing a black-
and-white world suddenly gone Technicolor.

The street was literally lined with men, chatting in
clusters, standing alone in doorways, sitting on stoops,
leaning against railings, strolling, everywhere. They
took no pains to hide their obvious interest in each
other. They seemed to eye each other with cool ease,
as if sex were merely a glance away. Dressed sensually
in clinging pants, an extra button open on their shirts
to reveal their chests, they seemed utterly unabashed,
saying what they pleased and acting as they liked. It
made me feel uncomfortable, self-conscious. I became
more aware of my body, which felt conspicuously fat
and frumpy in contrast to their carefully tended torsos.
I had known that Greenwich Village tolerated homosexuals, along with bohemians, artists, and Italian
grandmothers. But their freedom terrified me. Even if
I didn't look or act like them, I didn't want anyone to
know I was one of them. All my life I had difficulty
trying to prevent my eyes from lighting up whenever I
saw an attractive man. On this street it would be altogether hopeless. Just being seen in this company would
be accusation enough, and even a hint of suspicion
was as good as a verdict of guilty. I turned and practically ran back to the safety of my apartment.

It didn't take too many days before I poked my
timorous head outside my turtle shell for another look
at the wonders of Christopher Street. Within weeks

I knew neighborhood night life as well as I had known the parks and terminals of earlier years. I found enough sex, if not creativity, but I skulked around corners, afraid of being seen, especially once I found out that there were other English teachers at Staten Island Community College who lived in the Village.

One of them, Herb Liebman, lived only a few blocks away. He became my closest friend. He was only a few years older than I, but his life seemed more settled, his apartment more of a home than mine. We spent long hours discussing the state of the world, the neighborhood, the arts, and ourselves (except for one subject) over hundreds of coffees and cakes at his cramped kitchen table. Herb was craggily handsome though I wouldn't have told him so. His mind was swift and compassionate. He weighed issues with rabbinical complexity. His wife, Nina, was genuine and warm, always bustling hurriedly, forgetting this, accomplishing that, tending to their two young sons. Her patrician features were sharp, angular, pretty. With New Jersey behind me, I made Herb and Nina into surrogate parents and spent most of my time at their house. There were always friends dropping by to discuss politics and literature and employment and life. I spent several evenings a week engaged in such discussions at Herb's, a couple of evenings at home marking papers and reading science fiction novels about telepathic brotherhood and utopian futures, and a couple at NYU taking courses toward the Ph.D. One evening a week I went to the movies with Alice.

I tried everything I could to make it with Alice. At the doctor's behest I tried getting drunk, lying down with her, holding her, and nothing happened. We slept together, waking quickly in the middle of the night to take me by surprise. Nothing happened. So we went to the movies once a week, and we talked on the phone every day.

When my young cousin Grant came to stay for a couple of weeks on his way to become a rock musician, Uncle Arthur and his wife asked me to keep an eye on him. They had heard about the Village and all its drugs and dangers, but it turned out to be more a question of keeping the Village safe from Grant. He knew his way around. He taught me the secrets of marijuana. Smoking grass was something else. It opened new worlds of experiencing. I tried it with Alice. Nothing happened.

When I tried it and went to the local "tearooms," however, a lot happened. I left my telephone number scrawled in men's rooms of movie theaters all over the neighborhood, and occasionally my ads received an answer. A variety of men responded. Sometimes it was just a phone call, sometimes a quick "trick" at my place. And once it was a mind blower.

"Hello?"

"Uh, hi. You don't know me, but I found your number at the Loews Sheridan Theatre . . . in the, uh, men's room?"

"Oh, right," I answered. "Yeah, I left my number there."

"Mm-hmm," the voice said, warming up. "What do you like?" It was a familiar question. The S & M crowd is usually pretty blunt about asking who's going to do what to whom, at least for openers. The details are discovered with more subtlety.

"I like to suck cock," I said with equal bluntness, leaving the variations on the basic theme up to his imagination.

"That's usually the way I like it," he said. His voice had an intriguing mixture of authority and comfort.

"What's your name?" I inquired.

"Karl," he answered. "But that doesn't matter. You're

going to call me Master. In fact, you're going to call me Absolute Master. Try it: Absolute Master."

"Absolute Master," I said warily. I could have ended it by giggling and hanging up. But something made me want to play the game seriously. I wanted to be open. "My name is—"

"I don't care. You have no name for me. You are only an adjunct to my being. You exist only for my pleasure. Say it." There was a cruel edge in his voice.

I hesitated. Some sense of self deep inside me always made that part of the game difficult. No matter what role I choose, I still believe in my individual person-hood. But I like to test the boundary line between the rules of the game and my own integrity. That's what makes it thrilling. I answered meekly, "I exist only for your pleasure."

"Say it louder."

"I exist only for your pleasure."

"For your pleasure, what?"

"For your pleasure, Absolute Master." I hated it, but I loved it.

"Okay. I'll call you again. Be home tomorrow night at ten." He hung up without waiting for an affirmation.

I didn't stay home on purpose, but I was there anticipating it when the phone rang. He was calling from the opera house, where he was seeing a perfor-mance—with his wife! I had slept with enough mar-ried men not to be bothered by that. From the phone booth he promised all sorts of forbidden delights, de-livered all kinds of complicated instructions about what to do with my body in preparation for his visit. I pretended to comply.

It went on for over a week of phone calls at any time of day or night, filled with commandments, in-quiries, promises, until we finally arranged to meet at my apartment. I didn't know what might happen, but anticipating the unknown was also part of the thrill.

I opened the door to find an inconspicuous man in his forties with a touch of executive gray at the temples, dressed in plain jacket and tie. His quietly handsome face wore a surprisingly benevolent expression.

"Arnie?" he asked. I nodded. "My name is Karl," he said. There was no hint of the Absolute Master here. It was more like a visit from an uncle—the more usual kind of uncle, not the kind that runs in my family. Once we had settled ourselves over a drink, he began, "Did I upset you with the things I've been saying over the phone this week?"

"You sort of intrigued me," I confessed. "But I don't think I was too upset. I'm not sure I can really get into all those things you suggested though."

"Don't worry about it," he said. "We're not going to have sex. I just came over to talk with you about yourself." Not only was there no hint of the steel cruelty I had heard over the phone all week, but I sensed a distinct feeling of fatherly concern for me, a feeling I was confused by.

"You want to talk about me?"

"I was hoping that our conversations would reveal something to you about yourself. Do you think they did?"

"Nothing that I didn't know before," I said.

"Do you really want to do the things we talked about?"

"Not really. Well . . . maybe someday. Ah, I don't know. But something in the tone of your voice was turning me on to it." I answered the best way I could.

"Why do you write your number on bathroom walls?" he asked.

"To meet people."

"Don't you think there are better ways to meet people?"

"I haven't found any," I said.

"Maybe if you didn't depend so much on this sort of thing, you'd find some other ways. Where else did you leave your number?"

I told him.

"I want you to do something for me. Will you?" he urged.

"What?"

"Promise me first. Just trust me. I can command you to do it, you know." The steel edge glinted in his tone.

"Okay, I promise. What is it?"

"I want you to go to every place where you left your number and erase it. I'm going to check. And if they're not gone, your Absolute Master will call you again and make you do it."

The switching of the personalities within one sentence was frightening to me. "What does it matter where I leave my number?" I asked. "Why should you care?"

"Let's just say it's something I learned," he said, "something I feel an obligation to teach. Will you do it?"

"I guess so," I answered glumly.

He left with a cordial handshake. I didn't sleep very well that night, wondering what in the encounter had so confused me. He had violated some rule of the game, mixing his real self with his role, and so had I. But there was something quintessentially honest in that mixture of reality and fantasy, a truth I hadn't understood before. The next day I dutifully went from tearoom to tearoom and crossed out my own graffiti. That evening he called.

"I checked the places you told me, and the numbers weren't there. Good work," he said. "I don't think you need an Absolute Master now." He hung up.

I never saw him again, and yet I felt that I had been strangely commanded with love, as if Karl bore some message of compassion, something fatherly, even godly. I was disturbed by the encounter, no longer quite comfortable in my own skin. That was the first time I called the doctor between sessions to arrange an emergency visit to his office.

"Karl knew something you didn't," the doctor told me as I sat on the couch facing him, unable to lie down. "In a sadomasochistic relationship, it's the masochist's fantasy that's being acted out, the masochist who manipulates the situation. You let him see that your deepest fantasy was to be loved, not despised. He saw that you wanted to be cared about, protected. Being owned produces a secure feeling, like being somebody's child. A good sadist is paternal, a loving disciplinarian. Karl is an expert. He saw what you wanted and gave it to you, and the truth of your own feelings frightened you." His explanations made sense, but I understood them only intellectually. My feelings remained the same, jarred but unchanged. Yet I never wrote my number on a wall again.

The doctor shielded me not only from myself but from my mother. She had been snooping when I talked to her on the phone lately, trying to find out how my analysis was progressing, and I had told her little. She came to visit one Saturday, so I could tour the Village's antique shops with her and hop up to Saks Fifth Avenue and Bonwit's after my weekly appointment. But she insisted on coming to the office with me.

"I'll just wait in the waiting room," she said.

I acquiesced, silently suspicious.

On the way there she said, "I just want to say a few words to him, to find out how you're doing. It'll only take a minute."

"We have a lot to talk about today," I said limply.

"It'll only be a minute. I just want to see what he looks like," she insisted.

When we got to the doctor's office, he ushered me inside and blocked the door to the waiting room with his body.

"I just wanted to tell you how grateful I am for all you're doing for Arnold," she said unctuously. "And how is—"

"It was nice to meet you," said the doctor. "I must get to work now. Why don't you sit down and look at some magazines?" And he closed the door in her face. I applauded. "Some people require firm handling," he told me.

My mother didn't visit me too often after that. My father never visited. Our entire relationship was conducted on the telephone, except for once a year at the family's Passover seder. Few friends visited either. I spent more and more time alone, pacing slowly through a dreary routine of being a teacher all day and a graduate student some evenings and other evenings sitting at Herb's kitchen table or taking Alice to the movies.

One winter night, when it was cold and the snow lay dead where it had fallen on the city streets, I came home from school and hung my baggy black overcoat in the closet, tucking my academic-looking Persian lamb cap in the pocket where I wouldn't forget it. I said hello to my cats and opened my attaché case on my desk, setting aside the papers to be marked that evening. In the kitchen I put four pork chops into the frying pan: two for that night and two for the next night, so I could adapt myself to the family-sized packaging. I stared at the chops as they sizzled in the pan, and suddenly my life ground to a halt, just long enough for me to look at it. It was an epiphany. Pork chops and freshman papers and dowdy overcoats and secrets and cats and once a week at the movies. Was this to be my life? It just isn't good enough, I thought. It won't do.

I spent more and more time at Herb's, hiding from being alone. When summer came, and he and Nina took their family to Cape Cod, I was bereft. I sought solace in Heidi, their next-door neighbor, who had often come to visit Nina while I was there. She was from Vienna, the daughter of one of Hitler's soldiers. All of her friends were Jews, as if she sought to expiate her father's sins. She was currently awaiting divorce from an American she had met on an Israeli *kibbutz,* where she had lived one year. She was one of the most sexually appealing human beings I have ever encountered.

Her hair was dark blond and very fine, cut into precise bangs across her forehead and hanging with silken directness to her shoulders. Her features were needle sharp, but fragile. A quick blush rose to her cheek whenever she was pleased or angry. She blushed frequently, as easy with her emotions as I was clogged with mine. She was petite and boyishly small-breasted, and she was lonely.

That summer we went to the movies together, shared drinks at the local bars, and grew to like each other. Wherever we went, men admired her with their eyes and brought the color to her cheek. As we grew more comfortable in our friendship, she confided her sexual experiences to me, but I kept mine secret from her.

One evening Heidi came over to visit at my place. We talked easily while she savored the air conditioning. And as we talked, I began to notice her looking at me in a new way, a sexual way, and I was terrified. I tried to avoid her glance, to raise a new topic of discussion, growing flustered while she remained calm, talking lightly in her delicate Austrian accent, and all the while penetrating me with her steel-gray eyes. I felt my defenses slipping from me one by one, and finally I let go. I stood before her. She hurried into my arms, her voice catching as she murmured my name, and I held her close. She led me to my own bed, where I had slept futilely wth Alice and passionately with a host of nameless men. We slowly undressed each other, caressing and kissing all the while, and we lay down naked together. She modestly protected her small breasts with her slender forearm. Then we turned to each other, and nothing happened.

Later that week we tried it again at her apartment. And again nothing happened. I told her how sealed up I was, how exhausted I was, how unhappy I was not to be able to please her. She was comforting, understanding, or so she thought. I felt like a complete failure. I couldn't fuck Heidi or Alice or even any of the men I slept with. I didn't feel like much of a man.

The next week we both went to join Herb and Nina at Cape Cod. Each day she grew cooler and cooler, until it was as if the entire episode had never happened. We visited Provincetown, but even though it was staring me in the face, I didn't know I was looking at a gay gathering place. Everyone I talked to was straight. Homosexuality wasn't one of the usual topics of conversation. After two weeks I left to join Alice for a week on an island in Maine. We took separate rooms; we didn't even bother to try anymore.

That fall I sank into a deep depression. The doctor put me on antidepressants, and I found myself unable even to feel my own orgasms, which more and more occurred via masturbation and less and less in the company of another man. Heidi became my friend, turning me into a confidant, seeking my advice during her short-lived romances. I wrote moody poems, taught without enthusiasm, studied without interest. At the end of the year she came over to say goodbye. Her divorce had become final, and she had decided to go home to Vienna to live. When she left, I sat down and cried aloud.

I went on in my darkest mood for two more weeks, barely able to summon words from deep inside me all the way to my lips. Even Alice's concern was no use, and I was even less use to her. There was nothing that anyone could say or do. I went almost nowhere, saw almost no one. The weeks of intersession dragged on slowly, removing even what little human contact I had had at school, until even a trip to the corner grocery was more contact than I could stand, as if I were making a foray into some enemy territory. No music could be morose enough for me; no novel could take me far enough away and never end; the movies on television had lost their charm. Crossword puzzles and solitaire didn't take my mind off itself. And so I sat, the blinds drawn against the daylight, the lights off at night. I sat and tried to negate my own mind, to wipe out any trace of thought or feeling, to just sit, not moving if possible, so I wouldn't have to be aware of my body. I tried not to sleep. There were nightmares. I wanted to sleep without disturbance.

Herb kept calling to invite me over. Sometimes I managed to pull myself together enough to spend an evening in his kitchen, watching his family's life go by like a movie. And one night I went home wearily, barely able to lift my feet. My arm was almost too heavy to carry the key to the lock. I moved as slowly as one does underwater as I mechanically collected the sleeping pill samples I had been stealing from the doctor's desk drawer. I swallowed thirty of them, one by one. This time I had no note to write, nothing to say. I just wanted to sleep. I slept.

As if in a dream I struggled and writhed, feeling tied down, unable to move my arm. My arm hurt. The pain

was too strong for a dream. I opened my eyes to see
row upon row of fluorescent lights, and I thought, Oh,
my God, there's a heaven: there's no end! And heaven
looked like Franz Kafka's version of hell with its
officious rows of fluorescent lights. Lights? I thought.
I was alive. I looked down. My arm was tied to the
bed, an intravenous needle taped into it. Alice was
standing at the foot of the bed.

"Where am I?" I asked her.

"This is the emergency room at Bellevue Hospital."

"My arm hurts."

"They tied you down so you wouldn't shake the
needle loose."

"How long was I . . . ? What day is this?"

"It's Friday morning. You've been unconscious since
Tuesday night."

"How did they find me?"

"You were supposed to meet Herb to go to school
Wednesday morning. When you didn't show up, he was
worried because of the mood you'd been in the night
before. He got a policeman to break into your apartment. They pumped your stomach, and the doctor said
the only reason you weren't dead already was that you
had taken so many capsules that the plastic coatings
congealed, and the barbiturates were entering your
system more slowly than usual. They brought you here,
because all suicide attempts have to be brought here."

"I'm not very glad he saved me."

"I am," she said.

I was in the psychiatric building. They took away my
eyeglasses for fear I would break them and try to cut
my wrists, and most of what I saw was mercifully a gray
blur. Cigarettes could be lit only by the attendants, who
didn't especially like to be bothered. Flowers ended up
on the nurse's desk, like it or not. I was in a ward with
some twenty or so beds, each filled with some instance

of human misery and despair, sleeping fitfully through nights filled with babblings and soul-rending screeches. The hallways were lined with still more beds, more patients shuddering and moaning, some tied down, pleading in endless Spanish to be put into a chair or back into bed, unheeded for hours at a time.

I couldn't see the other patients as "they." It was "we." In spite of my education, in spite of my middle-class background, I had more in common with the inmates than with the keepers. When I went to the bathroom, I had more in common with the retarded adolescent squatting to shit in the next urinal than I did with the staff. The teen-ager and I both wore blue beltless pajamas. We both belonged somewhere else. The attendants wore more uniforms and seemed happy where they were, exercising their power over us.

I met alcoholics who were drying out for the thirtieth time, and listened to their stories of life in the gutter. I met zombies who walked in perpetual half-lives, paranoids pursued by shapeless monsters, people who had failed to cope. I had failed to cope too. We were all in the same boat. We ate our tasteless institution food with spoons, not to be trusted with forks or knives. When we shaved, we were watched by guards. We told each other our stories, trusting our kinship more than we trusted the impersonally polite doctors who kept their distance while we dealt with the callous staff. As patients we listened to each other's sorrow and comforted each other. As prisoners we traded secrets about how to get matches or how to hold up the elephant's pajama bottoms we had been issued.

I remembered Olivia de Havilland in *The Snake Pit.* I remembered Jan Clayton singing "Going Home." My wretched pork-chop existence looked good compared to this. Any life would. Our lives were permeated with gray. Piles of dirtied, bloodstained linens lay in open

heaps. Small mice scampered playfully all over the
floors. They frightened me at first, but the attendant
I told about them said, "You'll get used to it." Eventually they became a diversion. There was nothing to
do. All the pictures I'd seen of people in madhouses,
sitting in chairs with vacant expressions on their faces,
made new sense. There was nothing to do: a television
room with daytime hours to avoid upsetting shows and
no books or magazines. There was no glamorous occupational therapy, no melodramatic psychoanalytical in-
sights, only grayness. There wasn't even any point in
looking outside the barred windows. There was a garbage strike on, and our view overlooked a growing
mountain of the hospital's garbage. It was impossible
to look at it without thinking of the bubonic plague,
though it offered the only color aside from the visits
of friends: Alice, Herb, Gerry. They kept my spirit alive
with slender tendrils of reality that were all I had to
prevent me from joining the mad.

An intern interviewed me. He wanted to know why
I was there, why I had tried to die. I thought about it.
Was it loneliness? Heidi? Pork chops? Movies? Port
Authority? The answer had to fit into a box. If you
want to get out, you tell them what they want to hear.
"I'm a homosexual," I said. And medical science com-
piled another statistic.

I was there for five days that lasted forever. My doctor finally came to sign me out, a little disappointed in
me, but relieved that I had survived. Alice took me
home. I was amazed at the color that blossomed all over
the streets of New York, a city I had always thought
drab. I began to appreciate it all over again.

Everyone warned me not to tell my family. But I
couldn't resist. My mother showed up about a week
later.

"Don't you ever think of anyone else?" she asked. I

thought of her mourning for me. My heart swelled with hope for a new understanding, a new feeling, until she added, "Who can afford to bury you?"

This time I recovered more quickly. I had been through it all before. I went back to my life.

At first I spent most of my time alone. I frequented underground movies and avant-garde art shows and secretly savored their daring sexuality. I admired the new freedom of clothing and manner that the flower children were affecting. We listened to the Beatles together. I went to the first Central Park "Be-In" armed with two dozen daffodils. It was a head count to see how many people had begun to think the same way, and there were thousands, beaming at each other with big smiles, dressed in whimsy of Indian feather or fantasy of gypsy fringe. I felt old-fashioned in my tweed teaching jacket with its suede elbow patches. I went home with a handful of candy and two dozen daffodils fewer, but I went home inspired. Personal freedom was possible! At least long hair and fringed shoulder bags and jewelry were possible. I could wear them for freedom's sake. And if they happened to be feminine as well, I could tell myself that unisex was the latest thing.

It began with the professorial beard I had grown. I shaved it down to a moustache. My hair grew to the bottoms of my ears. On a visit to Herb's house one evening I tried wearing bell-bottomed sailor's dungarees with a chain belt and a tailored crepe shirt with full sleeves, a large collar and a plunging neckline exposing my chest. "You look like the guys who hang out on Christopher Street," Herb observed. "The neighborhood must be affecting you." I didn't wear my new look again for a month, but I continued more minor changes. Ties and jackets for school gave way to turtleneck sweaters, sometimes with beads. And each new little freedom I asserted made me feel ready to cope with the next. Besides, I had been so close to death that life seemed a lot less frightening. I bought pale-yellow-tinted glasses to brighten my perspective. I felt as if I were about to burst from a cocoon.

It was hard to sit still through the last of the courses for the Ph.D. I was tired of being part of what one teacher had called the student body: "a vast faceless amoeba." The people around me seemed so anxious to please, to be sure their term-paper margins were the specified width, careful not to offend their professors and to honor them, no matter what they thought. Once I had been afraid enough of them to leave school, and now they seemed so confined that I literally had to stifle angry screams in the classroom. I crammed for six solid weeks, jumbling *Beowulf* and Milton and Faulkner and "The Battle of Maldon" into enough evidence to pass my six hours of written exams. But that was the last I wanted to do. I had been going to add to the world's store of knowledge "A Comparison of Emily Dickinson and Frederick Goddard Tuckerman as Transitional Poets Bridging Transcendentalism and Realism," but it was hard to believe anyone cared. There was a new idea in the air. Education should be "relevant" to people's lives. I decided not to write my dissertation. I didn't want to be judged by values I no longer respected, a system that kept teachers and students in a pecking order. I wanted dignity more than I wanted credentials.

At least I don't have to pass it on to the next generation of students, I thought. I didn't have to make them compete with each other in order to educate them. "Professor Kantrowitz" evaporated. I asked them to call me Arnie. We sat in a circle instead of rows so everyone could see everyone else's face. I stopped giving tests altogether and began to experiment with the grades. And for the first time I began to listen to what my students were trying to say behind their grammatical errors. I felt I had more in common with them than I did with many of my faculty colleagues.

Those were the Vietnam years, the assassination years. Turbulence was in the times like the first gusts of a great storm, and I was caught up in events that were larger than myself. I felt like one of "We, the People," marching with hundreds of thousands to petition Lyndon Johnson for peace. I was tear-gassed with students in Washington, democratically. When we got home, we smoked grass together democratically and enjoyed the illicit status of "freaks" together. We marched around our own campus together, suspending classes in support of peace. We were innocuous enough, but we imagined ourselves on campuses across the nation, and we were sure we could hear injustice beginning to crumble throughout America.

In the summer of 1968, black rage burst in Newark. Frightened by the television accounts of buildings burning and bullets flying, I called my father to find out if he was all right.

"It's lucky I'm alive," he said. "I was driving the bagel truck, and I got caught right in the middle of sniper fire. The cops were on one side of the street, and the sniper was in an apartment building. So I see a cop trying to wave me back, and I think he means to stop, you understand, so I pull over. He jumped right into the cab of the truck, and he told me to get down on the floor, and there he is shooting right over my head." He waited to let the drama sink in, and before I could question, he continued, "They got him all right. There's still law and order, you understand, but the situation is such that you don't know if you're going to make it through the day." He waxed rhetorical, aware he had been speaking of History. "What did you have for supper?" he finished.

"Meat loaf." And I added, "How are Henry and Ruth?" before the subject became food.

"They're the best part," he said. "When I got home, they were upstairs on the floor of the kitchen. They could hear the shots, you understand."

"But they're all right?"

"They're all right. But the conditions here are such that we don't want to stay anymore. Ruth's nerves can't stand it. Shooting and burning, and who knows what's next? We're going to sell the house. Now that Pa's gone, you understand. . . ."

And so the house on Clinton Place was sold. It had housed my origins as a caterpillar. Ruth and Henry took neighboring apartments in Maplewood, a suburb of Newark, and my father moved to East Orange to live alone. My last ties to Newark had been severed. I turned my mind to other things.

I wasn't so sure I wanted violence, no matter how popularly preached it was. But I did want change. It felt like a personal victory when Lyndon Johnson chose not to run again. I decided to do my part by beginning to build the new world while others took care of dismantling the old. Along with two other teachers, some students, and some friends, I became part of Supernova, an experiment in education. We rented a loft among the artists' studios in Manhattan's SoHo district, and we hauled and hammered, painted and partitioned until we had a space where everything from macramé to modern dance could happen—silk-screening, poetry, photography, drama, ecology—and all of it could interact and crossbreed into new forms of art for the future. We got as far as silk-screening and photography, and I still wrote my own poetry, but none of it did any breeding. Still, it provided a happier part of my days than my furtive sex life did.

My days seemed split into several different lives: at home, in school, at Supernova, or visiting Herb. I was tireless through long days and secret nights, careful not to say the wrong thing in the wrong life. Being a freak was one thing. Being a queer was something else. The hippest of my friends still spoke of "faggots" with ease, albeit tolerantly. "Faggot" was generally the end of a discussion for me, never the beginning. I didn't want to reveal myself as different and inferior, or become the victim of the benevolent contempt with which I had heard them speculate on the subject. That would be bad enough. But if they found out I was a masochist to boot, I was afraid even the benevolence might disappear.

I didn't know what my friends would think of Jack, an "S" I'd met in a tearoom, who had conducted our relationship mainly on the phone between visits a month or two apart over the last couple of years. He would call me up and get his rocks off while he was talking to me. When he came over, he would get on the phone while I knelt silently, waiting for him to get it off. It wasn't love, but acting devoted was something I liked and needed. Our games would bolster his ego and assail mine, and that was fine with both of us. I felt a vaguely paternal security in Jack's commands, but what would my friends think of him? What would they think of the hustlers I bought and serviced in private ceremony, paying them to be actors in my masochists's play while I fed on their flesh with greed: the guys who stood on corners looking sultry until somebody came up with ten bucks, the guys who betrayed no emotion, the guys I met furtively walking the postmidnight waterfront streets after my friends went to sleep, casting my eyes to the ground whenever a straight couple passed, clinging proprietarily to each other amid our strangeness. I would look at my watch a lot, pretending to be waiting for someone who was late—*very* late since these scenes often occurred at 4 A.M. Pretending was second nature to me by then. I pretended affection for hustlers in private. I pretended in front of my students and colleagues and family and friends. I pretended in public, guarding my glance, so no one could see where it lingered. The only time I could act myself was when I was at home alone, which was often enough to make me prefer pretending.

One June night in 1969, I was on my way home from my weekly movie date with Alice when I passed what looked like the remnants of a crowd in Sheridan Square, two blocks from my house. It seemed like nothing to me, so I retreated home. I read in *The Village Voice* later that week that "the forces of faggotry" had staged a blow against the police who had raided the Stonewall Bar on Christopher Street. Parking meters had been uprooted for use as battering rams when the police had barricaded themselves inside, and someone had thrown a burning brand in with them. Only the last-minute arrival of reinforcements had prevented them from shooting their way out. Three nights of rioting had followed. I lived only two blocks away from History, and I had missed it. The *Voice* blamed it on the full moon and the death of Judy Garland.

A month later it was easily overshadowed by America's first landing on the moon. President Nixon called it the most important event since the invention of the wheel. In how many science fiction novels had I read the promise of the protective big brotherhood of a superior race from elsewhere? I watched the show on television, fascinated with the rare chance that there would be some sign of other life, some key to our origins or our destiny. But the choreography turned out boring, and there were no green people. Faced with the empty frontier of outer space, I found it difficult to stay awake.

The frontiers of inner space, however, were anything but boring. I went with Alice to see Timothy Leary at the Fillmore East, surrounded by slick showman's props, in this case a slide show as a psychedelic backdrop to pure white clothing and smooth rhetoric. He wanted hallucinogenic drugs to be the sacrament of a new religion. I didn't think we needed yet another religion, but there was a kernel of truth in what he said, something vaguely familiar, some sign of another life, some key to origins. I turned on, and I tuned in, but I didn't drop out.

I took my first mescaline trip as an experiment at home with a friend in attendance, but I didn't need much attendance. It was ten times what marijuana had been, frightening at first, until I relaxed and let myself enjoy it. I lay down and stroked my face gently. It was a thin veil between the internal and the external. It felt vague to my grazing fingers, the difference uncertain between what was me and what was not me, until I decided there was no real difference between them at all, except for appearance. I could feel myself growing larger. I could feel my cocoon begin to split its seams.

I was surrounded by space, a night full of stars with no center but my own vision. I was only my sight, unaware of the bed beneath my body or the room I lay in, unaware of having a body at all, conscious only of stars around me for 360 degrees. I felt as if I were everywhere, a consciousness dissolved into what I saw. But if I were everywhere, then I could be in no particular place. Where had my body gone? And my head? There was no head to have eyes in. There were no eyes, only vision. I fought back the welling paranoia, forcing my concentration into the field of stars.

Then I relaxed into a familiar feeling, the same feeling I had had from the bus window in northern New Jersey, and the same feeling I had felt beginning in the doctor's office years before. Only it was magnified ten times. I felt comfortable, trusting, as if I could embrace all the stars I could see. I felt at home. I don't suppose I was different when I returned, only much more myself than before.

In her own way Alice began to realize herself that year too. That summer's vacation in Maine was no honeymoon, and unable to contain their curiosity, the other passengers on the windjammer reminded us of that fact by asking us outright if we were married as we disembarked. "Just friends," we mumbled. By that fall it was clear to her that friends was all we would ever be. In the winter Alice took a vacation alone, and when she returned, at her request, we stopped seeing each other steadily.

In the beginning of 1970, with the consent of my doctor, I added group therapy to psychoanalysis in an attempt to survive. The group was run by another doctor with the latest techniques generated by places like the Esalen Institute. We would crawl on our hands and knees in the darkness, exploring the faces we encountered when we bumped heads. Or we would lie in a large circle, each head on the next person's belly, and close our eyes and say what we really felt about each other, or arrange pillows on the floor and trammel them with all the angers we felt for our fathers. Once we all undressed and discussed how we felt about our bodies. And strangely, the methods began to work! It was as if their way had been eased by the five years of understanding that psychoanalysis had provided. But analysis alone had been able to make me change neither my behavior nor my feelings, only my opinion. My analyst expected me to leap suddenly across a chasm, to exchange an old self-image for a new one. But only a cyclone could have pried my mind from the ledge it gripped. It was the only self-image I'd ever known. I couldn't let go until I had seen the new one. And I hoped the group would convince me, if not to leap, at least to turn and look.

I told them I was a homosexual and a masochist. They seemed to take it in stride. The doctor suggested that I needed to exert power. He arranged the group around me and told me I had to break my way loose. They closed ranks as if they meant business. I struggled and thrust to free myself with all the strength I had, and ten men and women used all their strength to contain me, pushing, resisting, until we were all exhausted at the same moment, and then I found some final burst of energy and emerged. I didn't know it yet, but I was a butterfly.

A few weeks later the cyclone struck.

6

On a sleepy Sunday morning I was doing the *Times* crossword puzzle and musing on the guy I had tricked with the night before. He'd just left with an invitation to see *The Wizard of Oz* on his color TV the next weekend. When I heard the doorbell, I wondered if he'd forgotten something.

Unable to see anyone through the peephole, I opened my door. As soon as I saw who it was, I tried to close it. He wedged his foot in the doorway, and his voice said through the opening, "I just want five dollars to get to Brooklyn." He was a hustler I had picked up two weeks before. I had seen him only once since, when he'd dropped by to ask for a "loan," which I'd refused. When he had left that time, I'd found my portable radio missing. He hadn't even been worth the original ten dollars I'd given him, lying back with his head cradled in his folded arms and acting as impassive "trade" to my fevered ministrations to his groin.

"Why don't you take the subway?" I tried to snarl through gritted teeth.

"I'm too tired," he nearly whined. "I need a cab."

I could tell he was a junkie. "Forget it," I said, with as much finality as I could muster.

"I know you're a teacher, and I know where you teach, and if I don't get my money, they're going to find out they have a queer working for them. Hand it over, faggot."

I tried again to shut the door, but it was no use. We wound up grappling in the hallway. He was stronger than I, but his drug addiction was in my favor. Finally, exhausted, I stopped and reached into my pocket, offering five dollars.

"Just take it," I said angrily. "But if you think you're going to blackmail me, forget it. I'd rather lose my job than support a punk like you! Get out of here."

"See you," he said, leering.

I looked up and down the hall, wondering if any of the neighbors had heard, but an apartment house in Greenwich Village is not very private. All of us had heard each other's personal life through our bedroom walls, which were transparent to the sounds of arguing and making love, and we were all professionally tactful in the elevators on mornings after.

That afternoon I was distractedly crossing Christopher Street when a leaflet was handed to me. It told a story that made me want to cry. The night before, the Snakepit Bar had been raided. It was an after-hours gay bar right around the corner from my house, and I hadn't known it was there. I had seen people going in and out of it at odd hours, but I had no idea what was in that basement, and I didn't want to know. The cops had forced their way in, seized all the money in the register, and arrested all 167 patrons. They had been taken to the Sixth Precinct house on Charles Street, and while they were being booked, one of them had tried to leap from a window ledge to the next rooftop to escape. He was a young Argentine terrified of losing his visa and being deported from this country, which was the punishment for homosexuals who visit America. He didn't want his family to know he was gay. He had fallen onto a spiked fence, his body pierced so thoroughly that it took nearly an hour to cut through the metal and take it, with him, to St. Vincent's hospital, where he lay near death.

The leaflet said that any way you looked at it that boy had been pushed. And he had been—by fear and ignorance and hate. I knew that he could have been me. My last resort in my worst fantasies was that if I were ever arrested, I would try to kill myself rather than face the shame of exposure. The homemade announcement on the leaflet was an invitation to a demonstration. Homosexuals would gather in Sheridan Square, march to the precinct house to protest the arrests, and then hold a deathwatch at the hospital. Why had it been handed to me? Did I look like a homosexual? I had been as careful as my desires would permit not to give myself away as I followed the progress of the new liberation movement with fascination, buying copies of *Gay* and hiding their headlines until I was home, under *The New York Times,* which never used to use nasty words like "homosexual." But it had nothing to do with me. I had too much to lose. There was no hope for my freedom. And now did some leafleter know me for what I was just by sight? Was there some crack in my mask, perhaps a wound that showed, unhealed from that morning's encounter with the blackmailer? It didn't matter. I had to see that demonstration. I had to know the difference between my terror and their courage.

A little afraid to go home because the blackmailer might be waiting in the hall, I went to see Teresa O'Connor, who teaches with me. She was at home with her husband, Aoki, a Japanese artist. I casually men-

tioned that a demonstration was going to pass their
door. (They lived right on Christopher Street, which
had always hampered my cruising because I had to
scurry around that corner with my collar up even if
Paul Newman's double was standing on the curb.)
Showing them the leaflet, I asked if they wanted to
watch with me.

We watched from across the street, following from
Sheridan Square to the precinct house to the hospital.
(The young Argentine lived. His body is scarred beyond hope; he wears a small bag under his shirt because his intestinal wounds made normal bowel move-
ments impossible.) There, safely across the street, with
a straight couple for camouflage, I heard the words
that changed my life. Five hundred homosexuals, not
timid faggots, but fierce, demanding, beautiful men and
women, were disrupting the nighttime stillness with
earthquake chants of "Say it loud: Gay is proud!"
Those words ate into my bones. Don't just say it apol-
ogetically, say it loud: demand it. Gay doesn't just exist.
It's glad to exist. It's proud. It's not only all right to
be a homosexual, it's a good thing! I couldn't believe it.
I had to believe it. It was true.

The next night was Monday, time for my weekly
group-therapy session. I told them the story of my
weekend, looking for answers, for support, for advice.
The doctor decided it was time for a psychodrama. He
arranged the group into rows to act as a class. Ralph,
the only other homosexual in the group, acted the part
of the blackmailer coming to threaten me in front of
one of my classes.

I began, "The assignment for next time is Chapter
Thirteen."

He approached the front of the room. "I was looking
for you."

"What do you want?" I asked coldly.

"You know what I want. I need some money. Let's have it."

"I have no money to give you, and even if I did, I wouldn't. Get out of here," I retorted as firmly as I could.

"Do you want me to tell these kids they have a faggot for a teacher?" he stage-whispered.

"I don't care what you tell anybody," I answered, my brow covered with real sweat. This was more than a psychodrama to me. It was a nightmare. It was my worst fear, and it felt as if it were actually happening. "Just get out of here," I finished. "Get out of my life."

The playlet ended there. The group agreed that I had said the right things, but that I lacked the proper strength of delivery. Maybe I should try yelling. I was in no mood for yelling. I was as tired as if I had just swum the English Channel with lead weights tied to my hands and feet. The doctor took a poll. The group agreed unanimously that the blackmailer would be back if I couldn't get tougher. Luckily he never did come back. I guess I had been tougher in the real situation than I could be in a play. But this had been no ordinary play. I had been traumatized by it. I spent the rest of the session in silence as the group turned to other matters. Finally, when the evening was ending, the doctor came over to me.

"How are you feeling?" he asked with evident concern.

"I can't explain," I answered, "but I'm feeling better, a whole lot better."

When I got downtown, I decided to stop at Teresa's house, just to relax my aching mind. We talked for a few minutes, when suddenly I changed the subject.

"You know why I asked you to come to that demonstration yesterday?" I began.

"What?" she asked, puzzled by the sudden change of topic.

"I asked you to come to that demonstration because I belonged in it, because I'm a homosexual, because I was afraid to go there without straight people to hide behind. I can't hide it anymore. I don't want to hide it anymore."

"That's nice," she said calmly. "Aoki and I have lots of gay friends."

"You do?" I was amazed.

"We figured that you were gay," she continued, "because we never saw you dating women, but you never seemed to want to mention it, so we didn't."

"Oh," I said, deflated. I had thought my mask was impenetrable, as most closeted gays do. They're the ones everyone else speculates about. There's not much to gossip over if the door is standing wide open for all to see. I went home, wondering what I had unleashed.

Jack, the telephone sadist, had of late been using my address to receive his raunchier mail, and he was coming over to pick it up at eight o'clock the next night. I knew I didn't want to see him anymore. There were newer, better things to do than prop him up at my own expense. But I was afraid, afraid that as soon as I opened the door, the old me would reappear. I decided to be out, to visit Teresa, but she wasn't home. It was already seven-thirty. Then I decided not to answer the door, but I knew I was copping out. I knew I had to confront him and get it over with. A little moral support would help.

I called my analyst and told him what I planned to do. He was ecstatic; just what he had been waiting for. He promised to call me back at twenty after eight—to provide an excuse if Jack were still there, to congratulate me if he had already been sent on his way.

He came on time. He got about three steps into the

apartment before I began. If I gave him any longer, I would be his.

"I have something to say to you," I said.

"Yeah," he said, not particularly interested. We had never conversed about anything, never let our roles slip. Only our fantasies related to each other, not ourselves.

"I'm not going to see you anymore. I'm in analysis now [I didn't mention the preceding five years], and I'm trying to be a person, a whole person. I want more than just adoring your feet: I want to make love to another whole person. Here's your mail. Please don't have any more of it sent here."

I had spent all my artillery in one statement. The rest was up to him. If he staged an argument, I would lose. I waited. He looked me over as if seeing me for the first time.

"Okay," he said, and he turned on his heel and left.

I was dumbfounded. Was this what I had been worried about? Was it really so easy to get what you wanted, simply by asserting yourself? I was no slave: I was Samson (maybe a little Delilah as well), I was Alexander the Great. I took a new look in the bathroom mirror. Maybe I wasn't as hideous as I had thought. Maybe if I lost some of the weight I had put on eating halvah and chocolate for supper in frustrated misery. . . . (I lost seventy pounds in the next year, dropping from a button-popping 196 down to a hold-my-stomach-in-and-pass-for-slim 126, a few pounds of which I later restored for warmth.)

The doctor called. I told him the story and listened to his praise.

Within five minutes the phone rang again. It was Jack. "You can't get rid of me just like that," he began.

"I just did, didn't I?" It was easy to be tough over

the phone. I knew that as well as he did; and besides, I had a new-found self-confidence to test out.

"You need me," he continued.

"I need someone who's a person, someone who wants to know me."

"I have something in my pants for you. You like it, remember?"

"I'm only interested if it's attached to a human being." I was growing imperious in my new strength.

"Don't you like my cock?" he asked, sounding almost wistful.

His cock. I had knelt before it . . . and then I realized that that was all I had ever done with it!

"Now that you mention it," I said coldly, "you never even let me touch the thing." My new perspectives were amazing me. This was getting to be fun.

"Well, you have to get to know someone first. . . ."

"It's been two years!" I was practically giggling. He stopped for a moment, regrouping his forces.

"You'll change your mind," he growled. "You need what I've got. I'll call you in a year, and you'll beg me to come and see you."

"I hope I'll still feel the same way then," I said flatly.

He hung up. I had seen the confrontation through to its end, and it had been worth it. I saw now that the telephone, the role playing, were defense mechanisms, used to ensure that there was no threat of genuine intimacy. I had been strong enough to confront him in person. He had been weak enough to have to run out to the nearest telephone in order to answer me. If I were stronger than he, if I could offer personhood as well as playing, then I had no place as his slave. I was a victor, not a victim.

He did call back—three times in the next few months. And each time my resolve was stronger. I never saw him again. But I've saved the S & M for occasional pleasure. The difference is that all of my partners are people to me, and I am a person to them. Adults need games as much as children do. Expressing my most private fantasies alone with another man, or with a few, is a way of sharing, a way of being honest, a way of making love.

The morning after I confronted Jack, I saw an ad in *The Village Voice* announcing a meeting of the Gay Activists Alliance. I had never liked going to meetings, especially with strange people. But maybe there would be something there that would explain what was happening to me. Maybe I wouldn't feel strange with these people. Maybe we had something in common. I had to know if they existed, or if what I had seen in the streets that Sunday had been a mirage invented out of my own needs. I had to find out if there was such an animal as a healthy, self-respecting homosexual. Maybe I could even become one if there was, by playing birds of a feather.

On Thursday I took a taxi to the Church of the Holy Apostles at Ninth Avenue and Twenty-Eighth Street. The meeting was in a hall attached to the side of the church. There were about sixty people there, mostly men, mostly white, mostly butch. But a handful of blacks and women and feminine men could be seen. The chairs were arranged in a semicircle facing a long table where a few people sat. I slipped into a back row, timidly hoping to observe the proceedings unnoticed. They spoke of the Snakepit demonstration I had seen and of their plans for petitioning the City Council. Jim Owles chaired with an aggressive insistency on the cause of gay rights that turned me on to it immediately. Wonderful people rose to speak, with anger, with philosophical wisdom, with cleverness, with strength. And each one was clearly an individual.

There were long-haired radicals and short-haired conservatives. No one was simply the stereotype I had been deluded into accepting, even in spite of myself as evidence. I had thought that I wasn't even any good at being a homosexual. I was learning that homosexuals, like every other group, are human beings, as different from one another as one would expect an Eskimo to be different from a Parisian. And I felt that I, who had never fully belonged to any group, always holding something in reserve because I hid the fact that I was gay everywhere except the analyst's couch and the waterfront streets at midnight, had at last found my people.

There was a lot of work to be done, and volunteers were needed to do it. I assumed I would only be able to work behind the scenes, perhaps offering my English teacher's skills in writing leaflets or statements, or at least in editing and proofreading them. I wasn't sure what I could do, but I knew I wanted to do something, and I knew that I would be back the next week. And somhow, when the list was circulated for volunteers to help gather signatures petitioning our City Council representative to work for our civil rights, I already felt I would be denying my best instincts if I failed to put down my name and phone number.

Saturday morning I received a call from Keith Robertson, a young social worker, saying he had been assigned to petition with me in Sheridan Square, right near where I lived. What had I gotten into?

If audience response counts for anything, Keith Robertson was the best-looking man in GAA: a well-turned-out five foot ten, with dark-blond hair that always seemd to fall in his bedroom eyes, leaving observers to bemoan the even momentary obscuring of his handsome features. When he spoke, he revealed a Middle Western simplicity and directness that was refreshing in cynical Manhattan. And so, accompanied by a sight most gay men (even considering the variety of taste) would be proud to be seen with, I took to the streets to fight for the rights that a week before I hadn't believed I deserved.

We stopped in the neighborhood store where I hadn't bought *Gay* because it was too close to home, and we received a warm reception and two signatures. After that I bought *Gay* there—without *The New York Times* to hide it in. We passed a friend of my cousin's on the street. I had always walked around the block when I was cruising near the antique shop she owned; but I was coming out of the closet, and my entire family would find out eventually. She gave us her signature, looking at me with surprise. It was all much easier than I had ever dreamed. My years of cowering had been unavoidable, but in vain.

The afternoon in Sheridan Square was a revelation. People were interested, amused, willing, rarely hostile. Neighbors, strangers, one of my colleagues from school: all sorts of people signed. But the moment that justified all of my internal *Sturm and Drang* occurred when a man of about seventy came up to me. As he signed the petition, he said, "This is too late for me, but I'm so glad it's happening. Maybe it will make your life better." I wanted to hug him and cry.

When the day's work was finished, Keith came over to me to say good-bye. Right there in broad daylight, under the glowing sun, in front of strangers and neighbors and heterosexuals, he kissed me good-bye—on the lips, and his lips weren't closed! I hadn't even considered that—the right to be more than verbally open, to be like other human beings, to kiss a beautiful man when you like and where you like. I walked home three feet off the ground.

That night I accepted the invitation to see *The*

Wizard of Oz. I felt like a different person from the one who had been invited only a week before. It turned out to be the first gay party I had ever been to in my twenty-nine years of closetry. Half a dozen of us watched Judy Garland's vulnerable innocence as Dorothy made her way to the Emerald City and back, daring to dream in Technicolor. I made new friends, and when the film was over, we went out to the Lower East Side (which in those days bore the Day-Glo label of "East Village") to a bar called The Hippodrome, where for the first time I saw men dancing with each other. Only then did I realize how, when I'd danced with women, I would lower my eyes if seduction seemed to threaten in theirs. It took me about two minutes to join the men at The Hippodrome, right up front, eye to eye, dancing with intent to fuck.

The gay world was a consuming infatuation, and liberation a vision we were reaching for, a vision of a world in which everyone could be honest, a world without pretending, where men could love men and women love women openly. Our Emerald City glistened in my newly shining eyes. Within weeks I moved from lonely pork chops in the frying pan to hurried sandwiches gobbled before or during GAA meetings. My life revolved around meetings. There was little time for anything else. I dropped out of Supernova, leaving educational experiment in order to devote all my spare time to "The Movement."

General membership meetings were at seven-thirty on Thursday nights, and the rest of the week was structured around that fact, with committee meetings and political intrigue and demonstrations interspersed. The weekly meetings were growing wildly, and along with them blossomed more and more committees dealing with every issue from pleasure to police. At first, small committee meetings were held in someone's apartment—mine, sometimes, if the group was small enough. Despite the conspiratorial air about our gatherings, we conducted our business according to Robert's *Rules,* and when we were finished, we relaxed our political selves and became people. That was how my consciousness got "raised."

We compared sexual notes, and I found that though my experience, like everyone's, is unique, I had a lot in common with my newly discovered peers. Among them I could at last feel "normal." GAA was anxious to avoid the radical style of its forerunner, the Gay Liberation Front, so there was never any actual consciousness-raising group. We were simply friends, clustering according to our interests, our politics, and our personalities. I made a host of new, gay friends, "brothers and sisters," who called me not Arnold but Arnie.

Jim Owles and Vito Russo and I soon formed a tightly knit triad, sharing fun and crisis and "dishing the dirt" on our mutual acquaintances with equal candor. Vito seemed a firefly, darting from meetings to movies he digested whole at the rate of several a day when he wasn't at work as a waiter. His brown eyes brightened with fervor at the mention of Judy Garland, pictures of whom adorned every room in his house—including the john. His soft round features stood ready with easy sentiment for all the celebrities who had acted and sung the fantasies I had grown up on. His wiry body hurtled more than it walked, forcing him to rush even when we were pacing a slow circle on a picket line. His tongue was sharp: "We're not 'girls,' lady; we're men who fuck each other, and you'd better get used to it!" His tears were quick when he was hurt, his smile radiant when he was pleased. We beamed at each other across rooms full of people like happy kids.

Jim was a more sober sort. He was the president of GAA, a good politician, angering some with his rigidity,

but refusing to surrender his firm hand to the sway of
fashion. His features looked pale and measured, yet
sensuous, his glance steady and clear. There was a military no-nonsense air about him: "Don't bother me with
your Sunday-school morality." But there was a person
beneath the surface that few people got to see. He bore
the burden of public position well—in public. In private
he wept over its weight. Our friendship was a love
affair without sex. We could walk with synchronized
strides. One of us proposed; the other disposed. We
played private games: sometimes the potentate and the
sage, sometimes Pinocchio and Jiminy Cricket, sometimes Harry and Midge, a typical suburban couple.
Midge's voice had a twang: "Harry, put on your
galoshes. It's snowing. If I've told you once, I've told
you a thousand times. . . ." Either Jim or I could play
Midge to the other's Harry, but they lived in private.
We would let Vito see them, but not the public.

In public we all showed our anger. Almost as fast as
I recognized I had any rage about the subject of gay
oppression, I was out in public airing it. Displaying
my emotions was awkward at first, but I had been encouraged in group therapy. I was being encouraged
here too, by Jim and Vito and a whole community of
new acquaintances to chat with on Christopher Street.
I was encouraged into doing things I had never imagined I could do. We shook Mayor Lindsay's hand in a
receiving line at the Metropolitan Museum of Art's
anniversary party, and we didn't let go until we could
say, "What are you going to do about civil rights for
homosexuals, Mister Mayor?" I probably sounded more
like a reporter than a revolutionary, but I felt like a
revolutionary, defying my own timidity in order to
change the world as suddenly as I had changed my
mind. Our sense of community allowed us to do more
and more outrageous things. We encouraged each other

into more and more nonviolent "zaps": into dancing together in front of a crowd of straight people in Central Park and into disrupting the taping of the mayor's television show.

Letting out the anger was never easy for me. It was embarrassing. But letting out the pride was a pleasure. My favorite demonstration was simply holding hands in the streets. We kissed hello and good-bye wherever we went; we held hands and embraced as lovers and friends. Strangers rarely let us know they noticed, but when I walked behind a couple of men holding hands, I could see people turning to stare and trade nervously amused looks with each other. Holding hands in the street took all the strength I had. It's difficult not to be self-conscious when first you flout custom. But as part of a gay crowd I could yell "Two-four-six-eight: Gay is just as good as straight" with a feeling I'd never had when I'd yelled "Peace! Now!" I had never worn political buttons, but buttons were in style along with politics, and I wore the gay liberation lambda symbol as a matter of honor, just hoping people would ask what it meant, so I could tell them. Even when there wasn't a man's hand there to hold, I wanted to make my gay presence real wherever I went.

I maintained a dwindling interest in other causes. Ralph, the other gay man in group therapy, came along when I went to spend the weekend in Washington for the 1970 annual peace march with a group of gay friends, all of us huddled together in the back of a chugging Volkswagen bus. Along the way I got into a little foreplay with someone named Bob, and we spent the night together. The peace march the next day was as much a picnic in the park as it was marching and oratory. It was definitely not a popular uprising. Our gay contingent drew plenty of surprised stares but few comments, even as we relaxed on the lawn with a little more than fraternal closeness. My head was comfortably ensconced in Bob's lap, looking up at the sky, our friends in similar postures strewn around us. Slowly, out of the corner of one eye, I realized that not only was Bob stroking my brow with one hand, he was holding Ralph's with the other. Still accustomed only to anonymous contact, I was just beginning to have sex with the same people I mixed with socially, and I didn't know how to behave. Then they excused themselves to go for a walk. I was so angry I went home in another car.

I arrived at group therapy the next night just in time to overhear Ralph confiding to one of the other patients, "I stole a trick from Arnie in Washington yesterday." The people in the group had become used to our being open. We had taken to sitting with our arms around each other during sessions, which had established us as comrades and as different. His gloating turned immediately to red-cheeked embarrassment when he saw my angry face in the doorway.

"I was just. . . ." he tried to explain.

"I know what you were 'just,'" I mimicked, "and I don't think it's very cute."

We began the group discussion with what had happened to us the day before. Everyone listened patiently for a while, and then they passed their judgment. It had been my fault for not asserting myself, for not saying to Bob that I minded what he was doing, for not reminding Ralph of my feelings. Ralph and I had a good deal to work out. He had sexual feelings for me that weren't mutual. The others lost interest and drifted away piecemeal to discuss other matters, eventually reforming as a circle in another corner of the room. It wasn't long before Ralph and I had resolved our problems and glued together a cracked friendship.

"I wish the others could have seen how we resolved

our feelings," I said. "What are they doing over there anyway?"

"They're busy with their own problems," he said. "They probably thought this was just a homosexual bitch fight. *Fuck them!* I'm not staying after the two of us are finished."

"I'm angry too," I said, "but I want to stay. Walking out won't make the message clear." I wanted to be different but not separate, and I wanted the rest of them to know it.

We kissed lightly, and he left without saying a word to the others, who were so busy they didn't even notice him go. I went to join them, standing at the edge of their seated circle.

"Where's Ralph?" one of them asked, noticing me.

"He left because he was insulted," I said.

"Did you fight?" he asked, hesitating a moment as if he feared another installment of soap opera.

"No. We worked out our problems directly. He left because *you* insulted him, all of you. And you insulted me too."

"I don't understand," the doctor said. "I thought we listened to your story."

"The story wasn't the point. The resolution of the problem between us was. And that's where all of you ignored us. It's not even something we take personally. It's something we're used to as homosexuals. For the first time in this group something real happened between two members—out there, in the real world." I felt the authority born of just grievance, and they obviously felt it too. They were all listening raptly. "It's easy to be in this room and discuss things like why somebody chose to sit in a certain place. But it isn't easy to cope with a real situation. Something important was happening between Ralph and me. What you all did by walking away was to tell us our situation wasn't real, and there's only one possible reason for that. It's because we're gay. You ignored the real feelings we were working out as people, because you decided that gay people's problems with each other weren't your concern. Well, you're wrong. Problems are problems, and people are people, and what happened between Ralph and me could have taught you all something, but you blew it, all of you. You blew it because you're prejudiced. You think our lives are just imitations of yours and that our feelings aren't real. Well, I'm telling you they are. I'm standing right here in front of you, and I'm a real human being, and I'm a real homosexual, and I'm a real angry man. Put yourself in my place. Now are Ralph and I equal members of this group, or aren't we?"

The whole group stared at me in wide-eyed silence. Nobody had ever talked to them like that before. And I had never talked like that to anybody before. My feelings were coming out at last, and they were more powerful than I had imagined. They were so intense they scared even me, but I liked them already. I felt stronger than ever before.

Finally the doctor spoke. "You're right," he said. "The only thing we can say is that we're sorry and it won't happen again." A few people seconded. No one demurred. I sat down. I was a victor.

So when Jim asked me to run for the secretary of the rapidly growing GAA, I let him talk me into it. It was a campaign that won points for its modesty. My opponent was Keith Robertson, the man who had first kissed me on the street. I was afraid his handsome face would outweigh my academic background. There were cries of "Take it off" whenever he stood to speak.

I accepted the nomination with honest fervor: "I believe that GAA has done something for me and now I'd like to do something for it." In spite of myself, I was

elected. I had become a politician. I felt like a dignitary
as I dressed for the first gay pride march on a bright
Sunday in June, 1970. It was the first anniversary of
the Stonewall riot, and we wanted to commemorate it
as our own St. Patrick's Day, Steuben Day, or Columbus
Day in New York. We were going to have a parade.
We would leave our Greenwich Village "ghetto," where
our numbers made it safer to be gay, and march up
Sixth Avenue, through parts of Manhattan less tolerant
of our lifestyle, to Central Park, where we would hold
a "Gay-In." The number of people who appeared would
matter to me much more than the head count at the
Be-In I'd attended at the same site a few years before.
The future of The Movement depended on it. Gay activists claimed to represent a mass of invisible constitu-
ents, and we needed their appearance to prove it. So I
was nervous as I spread an array of political buttons
across the chest of my gay liberation lambda T-shirt:
"Gay Is Good," "Gay Revolution," "Fellatio."

We were gathering along Waverly Place because there
weren't enough of us to rope off Christopher Street for.
I was going to be a marshal, which added to my ner-
vousness, since the rudiments of nonviolent crowd control taught to us the day before by a team of Quaker
pacifists didn't seem certain of containing the hostility
we might meet along our way. I put on my red arm-
band and went out to meet my date, Donald Shaug-
nessy.

When I got to Waverly Place, only a few people were
milling around. Marty Robinson was an energetic
carpenter who articulated our dream handsomely: "The
'cure' for homosexuality is rebellion." He was there
ahead of me. I kissed him hello.

"What do you think?" I asked him.

"It's still early," he said with nervous rapidity.

"Do you think there'll be enough?"

"I'll be happy if we get a few hundred," he said reassuringly. "If that's who's willing, then that's who'll march."

"But we've notified the media and everything. We'll look silly with only a few people."

"It's a celebration, not a zap. Why shouldn't people come? Do you know how many gays there are in Manhattan alone? They'll come."

Nobody knew how many gays there were in Manhattan. The Movement claimed 10 percent of the population, based on Kinsey's statistics, but who listens to Movement figures? For blocks around, people were sprinkled in small knots, waiting to see who was going to march and who wasn't before they committed themselves, but slowly more and more gathered behind the police sawhorse on Waverly Place until we had several hundred.

"Maybe we announced too early a starting time." I greeted Donald, kissing him at the same time.

"They'll come," he said.

"But we've been having events all week. People are tired, and it's Sunday morning besides. What self-respecting homosexual would get up before noon on Sunday? It would look like he—or she—went home alone after last night's dance, as if that weren't exhausting enough!"

"Don't worry," he calmed.

By noon, when we were scheduled to start, we were packed along Waverly Place for two-thirds of a block. It looked like a little over five hundred to me. I was more disappointed than elated, but I was damned if I was going to show it. Whatever we were, we were going to be proud of it. We started along the sidewalk, because we didn't have a street permit. But within blocks, with cries of "Out of the closets, and into the streets," we took to one lane of Sixth Avenue's easily diverted traffic.

Balloons went up. Signs appeared in the crowd: "HI, MOM," and "BETTER BLATANT THAN LATENT," and "I AM A LESBIAN, AND I AM BEAUTIFUL." The Mattachine Society, which had been working to help homosexuals while I was back in high school, held clusters of small flowered signs. The Gay Liberation Front raised its white banner, adorned with large pairs of same-sex symbols, lovingly linked. Donald and I marched with the large blue-and-gold lambda banner of GAA, our arms around each other.

Curious crowds began to string along the sidewalks as we passed up the avenue, flaunting our hearts on our sleeves. There were smatters of giggles, but they were quickly stifled. We were a few too many to offend. The spectators' faces showed amazement, confusion, shock, resignation, unconcern, affirmation. Ours showed two emotions: pride and determination. We were coming out of our closets, however many of us could, but we were coming out together.

At Fourteenth Street I passed my psychoanalyst standing quietly at the curb, smiling. I ran up and kissed his embarrassed cheek, and he introduced me to his lover of nearly thirty years.

"Join us," I invited. "Out of the closets and into the streets!"

The doctor shook his head. "Not in my profession," he said. I sympathized, but I ran back to my place in the march. Within the month both my doctors agreed that I was healthy and ready to cope, and both analysis and group therapy ended.

I could see for a few blocks ahead and a few behind that the march was moving in a narrow but steady stream. When we got to the Chelsea Flea Market, shoppers abandoned their bargains to line the curbs and stare. Students waved good wishes at us from the window of their ballet school. Construction workers did an enigmatic jig high above the street. At Forty-Second Street a stern-faced Bible thumper held aloft a sign that warned: "SODOM AND GOMORRAH." And we chorused, "Out of the closets and into the streets," and "Out of the theaters and into the streets," and "Out of the bars," and "Out of the stores and into the streets." At Radio City a line of men stopped to do their impression of the Rockettes' chorus line kicks. A few blocks later a self-styled "Fairy Queen" appeared at the head of the parade—some guy dressed in a tulle gown and a golden crown and wand, looking like Billie Burke as Glinda the Good Witch of the North, with everything but the pink bubble. When we got to the entrance of Central Park, we jibed, "Out of the bushes and into the streets," which, given the park's reputation, may well have flushed a few blushing guys out, zipping up their flies.

At last we came to the Sheep Meadow, our feet hot and tired. I got to the crest of a small knoll before I turned around. There behind us, in a river that seemed endless, poured wave after wave of happy faces. The Gay Nation was coming out into the light! There was hardly a dry eye on the hill. What had begun as a few hardy hundred had swollen all along its route, until we filled half the huge meadow with what the networks and newspapers estimated as five to fifteen thousand people, all gay and proud of it!

We needed a rest. Somebody started a chant: "Everyone standing is straight!" and thousands of people sat down where they were. We began to hug and kiss, to show off our clothes and take off our clothes, to play games and sing songs and begin that night's lovemaking early.

Donald and I wandered around, visiting friends, playing, stopping to embrace. Beneath a tree at the meadow's eastern edge lay two male couples who had been there since dawn locked in one long kiss, breaking the heterosexual world's record. I wandered among the crowd. There were men who wore dresses and women who wore denim overalls. Some wore their faces painted and sparkling with glitter. Some were utterly plain. Fanciful costumes were here and there amid the prevailing blue jeans: costumes made of shredded crepe paper, or dripping with rhinestones, or patchworked a hunderd motley colors.

We were leathermen and cha-cha queens, and we were glad bright-eyed women with flowing manes, black transvestites and young Orientals and a few old faces; we were gentle bicycle riders and proudly strutting superstuds, questing wanderers, fierce feminists, revelers and rioters, seers, politicians, artists, cowboys, philosophy teachers, husbands and lovers, loners, pot heads and patriots. We were transsexuals and opera queens and Judy Garland fans and hardhats and hairdressers and poets and fops, and we were totally honest poseurs. We were panhandlers and executives, mothers, anarchists, veterans, bank robbers, barflies, Catholics, and at least one twenty-nine-year-old Jewish Assistant Professor of English from Newark, who was having the time of his life. Arms linked, the legions of gays were marching to Oz. We were off to see the Wizard. We were coming out.

7

I DIDN'T OPEN THE CLOSET DOOR TO AN ALL SINGING, all dancing, all Technicolor welcome. It took many months and a lot of encouragement from my new friends. Surrounded by each other, it seemed that if we told the truth together, the world would change. "Just tell the truth," my mother had taught me. No longer alone, I was less afraid. So I set about becoming honest and changing at least my corner of the world, and I assumed that the Emerald City was not far off.

Coming out was a little different with each person. The women were generally easier to tell, expressing their relief with responses like, "Thank goodness you're something. I never heard of you going out with anyone, and I thought you were asexual!"

The men were a little more intimidating, but I didn't let that stop me. One of my colleagues answered my declaration with, "I thought there were some queers in the department. Do you know any others?" But his tone was sympathetic.

"If I did, I wouldn't tell you," I answered. "They'll

have to do it themselves. And the word isn't 'queers.' It's 'homosexuals.' Try to remember that."

When I made my announcement to Herb, he said with concern, "What are you trying to do? Destroy yourself? Why do you have to tell everyone your secrets? Do you want them to hate you?"

I answered, "Do you hate me, Herb? Do you hate me because I'm gay?"

"You're my friend," he said simply.

There was sporadic hassling after that, when he would inadvertently drop words like "cocksucker" in my presence, but a little rage cleared that habit up.

My childhood friend Gerry, at whose wedding I had been the best man, confessed it made him uncomfortable. "It's just an emotional reaction. Give me some time to get used to it." I gave it. He got used to it. I told his parents. His father received it as a civil rights issue. His mother didn't much like the fact, but she loved me, and welcomed me in her home as always.

From other old friends there were confused silences, unanswered letters, doubts and qualms from people who I thought knew me so well that no such news could alter our relationships. One friend, Louis, told me it was fine with him. I had driven his wife to the hospital when she was in labor, and I was his daughter's godfather. But the first time he saw me kiss a man hello, he fled the apartment in embarrassed confusion, tripping over his own excuses.

"I was paranoid," he explained on the phone a few days later. "It touched something inside of me that I don't want to know about. I'm really sorry. We'll get together again." I haven't seen him since.

But I had no time for everyone else's pain. I worked on the premise that anyone who couldn't deal with the fact that I was gay never really knew me in the first

place, liked only part of me, and all of me was going
to be up front from then on, ready or not.

Approaching my mother about the subject for the
second time wasn't easy. I didn't want any more salt
on my head, and her repugnance for the topic had put
it in a class with leprosy. I hadn't seen much of her
lately. The dream life she had forged for herself had
begun to crumble. The heavies were muscling in on my
stepfather's numbers territory. At the same time, with
startling regularity, customers were winning their numbers bets, forcing him to pay out what would have been
his profits. My mother and he had invested their earn-
ings in stocks, but the market was in a slump, and
instead of being able to pull out their investment, they
lost tens of thousands of dollars, money that might
have gone to save the business. The rest had been spent
on the house that crested Athens Road in Short Hills.
The house had become a millstone, until it seemed
worth consideration to insure it heavily and fire-bomb
it. Instead, Frank borrowed money from the under-
world and then found he couldn't pay it back. The
Mafia had been known to strike at home and family
to intimidate its debtors. They had to flee. They sold
the house and went into hiding in southern New Jersey,
not answering the phone, receiving mail at an anonymous post office box. The furniture—rugs and silver
and crystal and paintings, the lavender brocades, the
statues and busts, the silk chairs and the seventeen-
foot couch—all went into storage without insurance.
There was a fire in the warehouse. Nothing remained
but ashes and memories of grandeur and a return to
bitterness. The Cadillacs were aging, the furs were looking worn around the edges, and the eleven-carat diamond ring that was my mother's most precious
possession was in a pawnbroker's shop. They needed
the money for food. Frank had lost all of his incentive

and sat around waiting for something to happen. Occasionally he played solitaire.

So my mother was in none too receptive a mood
when her older son declared that he liked being a homosexual. "I've found out that homosexuality isn't a sick-
ness after all," I announced. "It's no different from
being left-handed in a world that's full of right-handed
people. It's not a question of failure on your part; it's
just the way some people are, and they can . . . *we* can
be as happy as anyone else. I mean, I don't think I
want to kill myself over it. I'll just be healthy my own
way, like my friends."

"If that's what makes you happy," she said, leveling
her gaze at me like an antiaircraft gun from the chair
where she sat. "But you wasted all that money being
psychoanalyzed for nothing." The subject was closed.

"My brother's response was more equivocal. "I
guess I always knew it," he said quietly, "even if I never
said it to myself in so many words."

"Then it's okay with you?" I asked, not seeking approval but friendship.

"I won't condemn it, but I can't condone it," he
answered.

But I wouldn't accept mere impartiality. "It's not up
to you to judge me," I said. "That's not offering very
much."

"What do you want me to do? Throw my arms
around you and be glad I'm your brother?"

Fifteen minutes later I thought of an answer. "I won't
ask you to throw your arms around me," I said with
steel determination, "but is it too much to expect you
to be glad I'm your brother?"

"Don't get excited. I'm glad. I'm glad," he answered.
He looked at me in a new light. "It's just that I have
to think about it."

I told my father next. I had heard stories of fathers

disowning their gay sons, breaking their arms with wrenches, committing them to asylums. But talking to him on the phone one time, I simply let it happen. I had been telling him about an argument I was having with my mother.

"Don't let your mother rule your life," he counseled. "You have to live by your own rules."

"I do live by my own rules, Dad. But I'm not sure you would approve of them either."

"I know what you are," he answered to my amazement. "I see how you live." (I had never thought of my pork-chop lifestyle as especially exotic, but Greenwich Village spoke for itself in his New Jersey mind.) "And I still say live by your own rules," he finished "as long as you're not hurting anybody."

What an easy relief. Why hadn't this happened earlier? But I had to be sure we were talking about the same thing. It wouldn't be a genuine coming out if I didn't say the words loud and clear. "I'd rather have you know I'm a homosexual than have to hide it," I asserted. "And you'd know sooner or later anyway, because I've become very active in the gay liberation movement."

"Can't you keep your name a secret?" he asked worriedly. "What about your job? The situation is such, you understand, that you have a lot to lose. Let somebody else do the demonstrating, somebody who doesn't have a career like yours." This was in accord with his general "Don't make waves" school of political apathy.

"There is nobody else," I answered. "It's my struggle. We all have something to lose—and something to gain. Don't worry about me: I'll survive. My self-respect is more important to me than my job anyway."

Remembering my father's admonition awhile later, I was a little nervous when President Birenbaum of Staten Island Community College showed up at an En-

glish Department party. I knew I was wearing my
lambda button as I went up to greet my boss, but
principle came before security. The first thing he said,
pointing to the button, was "And what's this?"

"It's a lambda," I replied cavalierly. "It's the symbol
of gay liberation. I'm a homosexual, and I'm working
in the gay movement."

He looked a little startled, but suppressed it almost
before I could notice it. Then he touched my cheek
gently with his hand. "Good luck," he said.

"And I'd like you to meet my friend Jim Owles, the
president of the Gay Activists Alliance."

He remembered to find us before he left, and to say
good-bye to Jim by name. Presidents go in for other
presidents. It doesn't matter what they're presidents of;
they respect the politician in each other.

For the first time in my life I felt sure of who I was.
I was still an English teacher at school, but I became a
gay English teacher. I was still the son and brother and
nephew and cousin everyone had known, but a gay son,
a gay brother. I was still some sort of Jew, not in the
arena of the synagogue perhaps, or in the bosom of the
family, but from memories of childhood bowls of chick-
en soup and Grandpa Simon's tales of life in the Russian *shtetl,* and from the ineradicable image of the gas
chambers. But I was a gay Jew. All day I was the same
person. Before all of my identities, in whatever situa-
tions I found myself, I was a homosexual first and anything else second. I was professionally gay.

Coming out into the gay world, I encountered the
ironies of my own past. At demonstrations or meetings,
at bars or on the beaches of Fire Island, I have met
representatives from each school of my life: from gram-
mar school, high school, college, graduate school, and
the schools I've worked in—both teachers and students.
Always there is the moment of surprise, and then the

thought: *Of course, the way he used to hang around my desk and notice the same men who turned me on;* or, *Now it all makes sense, the way she spoke of women.* Sometimes there was a note of embarrassment in the other person at being discovered. Sometimes there was a sense of kindred relief. The difference was liberation.

Chin held high and hopes higher still, I declared my solidarity with my people. Solidarity is not just a unioneer's catchword. It is a sense of belonging I have felt to my marrow, a kinship as thick as blood relation. I shared with the members of GAA a single purpose in which I trusted and a single passion to which I surrendered myself. We shared the sacrament of honesty, our coming out. Together we were something significant. We were a part of History, and we knew it. In our minds we were a people struggling valiantly to shed the bonds of oppression, and for every one of us who dared to come out, there were hundreds, no, thousands waiting their opportunity to join us.

At first I didn't even have to leave my apartment to move to a new world. I could simply open my door and let the gay world in. My cramped quarters were centrally located, and the doorbell was always buzzing with people dropping by to share a joint or some of the latest "dish" or a little political intrigue. There was always something to accomplish, someone to be with, a sense of purpose and meaning to every moment. My old, lonely self was forgotten in the rush of activity. My old book friends lay gathering dust. I rarely had time to clean, because instead of contemplating things, I was busy doing them. I stopped writing complicated experiments in moody poetry, and I began writing gentle love lyrics, gay love lyrics, expressing for the first time my true experiences and my real fantasies. The truth, as always, was exhilarating. All of us danced in it. When you have had a secret all your life, it is a considerable refreshment to air it to death. We spent our days and nights coming out, liberating ourselves, carving ourselves a larger psychological territory to live in. Our fervor was messianic, but we were marching to Emerald City with oddly scattered steps, some of us seeking to change the world, some of us seeking to change ourselves, some of us seeking both. We didn't all agree about what liberation was, let alone how to get there.

Some theoreticians held that the "barsandbaths" (pronounced as one word in their lexicon) were oppressive institutions where we treated each other as sexual objects rather than as human individuals. But I had never ventured to explore those experiences, and my first forays into them seemed like liberation to me.

Before I came out of the closet, I had only been inside a gay bar one daring night, a summer earlier, in 1969. Provided with a list by my solitary gay friend, Leslie, I had ventured into three Village bars, entering and exiting each of them furtively, afraid of being seen in their doorways. The first held clusters of middle-aged men in casual sweaters, having a quiet neighborhood drink. I stood alone in the corner and hurried through my gin and tonic. The second catered to a variety of younger men in clean dungarees. The jukebox was very loud. It was crowded. I stood alone in the corner and hurried through my gin and tonic. The third was a leather bar down by the waterfront. Though I was accustomed to S & M, I had never dressed like a cyclist, and I felt like a petunia in a cactus patch. I stood in the corner and hurried through my gin and tonic, and then I stumbled my drunken way home alone.

Among my new movement friends my self-confidence was bolstered. I could go out for a drink, soon learning a nonchalance that was studied, but which masked my shyness. Being cruised by the men in bars made me feel something like a lamb chop in a butcher's window. I had to affect a pose if I wanted to be like the others, to pass myself off as the lumberjack of somebody's sexual fantasy or the pirate of someone's dreams. But I was dripping hair past my shoulders and sprouting a garden of jewelry: a cameo at my throat and a forefinger ring and a few bracelets. I wore orange lenses in my eyeglasses since I had grown jaded with a mere sunshine-yellow view of the world. My dungarees blossomed with rhinestones and embroidery. My femininity was declaring an end to its political suppression.

I looked around me with solidarity. But except for the daily patrons, solidarity is not what people go to gay bars for. They go to get laid. When I went out to the bars, I kept my political femininity to a whisper—no more than a single bracelet or a kerchief in my pocket—and I wore my pants a size too small, so I could outline my "basket" of genitalia seductively. I understood what the liberationists meant. I was uncomfortable. How could I spend all day coming out of my closet and spend all night in a new deception, pretending to feel the gruff callousness that secretly attracted me when I saw it in others? When I was horny enough, I figured out how. Whatever my politics, I had every intention of getting laid.

There was always a bar of the season. Sometimes they took themselves with a dash of humor, hanging a sign in the men's room saying, "Employees simply must wash hands and things before setting one boot outside this room!!" In most the decor is serious, the lighting vague, the jukebox loud enough to prevent any intelligible conversation, reducing most contact to the purely visual. Frequently there is a mirror over the bar that helps you to determine whether the guy you've been looking at covertly is looking back at you when you're not looking because he doesn't want you to know he's looking at you until he's sure you're looking at him through your shaded glasses. If no one better-looking gets in the way, you might edge through the crowd, trying to spill your jostled drink only in between people's ankles and not on their boots. It has always been my social misfortune, from college parties to gay bars, not to like beer. Learning how to hold on to my Burgundy butchly in a stemmed wineglass while navigating through a sea of elbows took practice, like negotiating about sex with a stranger while looking over his shoulder for a better possibility. I kept on trying, but it was as if I had traded in one charade for another. Nonetheless, that's where the men were at, and that's where I was going to be.

Most of the sex generally happened when the bars closed. Some went off to the after-hours bars that featured orgies in their back rooms. The rest returned to lurking in the doorways. I lurked with a new assertiveness. Standing in doorways was an open eroticism I had never dared. It was freer than scurrying around corners nervously, yet it was still presenting myself not as a person, but as a thing. My self-conscious masculine posture got me laid some nights. Other nights I felt like a crushed blossom. But I stood my ground in those doorways, often past dawn. I was out there trying to meet my Mr. Right, the man with Clark Gable's eyes and Laurence Olivier's genius and Spencer Tracy's patience. He would have a proud physique and a pirate's beard. His stream of fascinating conversation would never run dry. He was Rhett Butler and Heathcliff rolled into one. He was my father perfected. He had Superman's unerring awareness of others' needs and King Arthur's noble politics with a humanitarian bent to the left. He could be a philosopher lumberjack with a mountain cabin; but a wise carpenter like Grand-

pa Simon would do, or a poet from a hippy commune,
or a brooding artist of ideal principle and consummate
skill. But whatever else he was, he had to be dedicated
to my adoration of him so that our union could be perfect. Nothing less would do. Like my mother I deserved something special. I wanted for my perfect lover
none other than the Wizard of Oz himself, and I was
looking where he was least likely to be found: in the
mirror of a dimly lit bar.

The Movement's approach to the bars had to do
with breaking the Mafia's stranglehold that kept all of
us in a bind between their exploitation and the police
department's harassment. We needed alternatives, and
we had to make our own. We also needed money. So we
solved both problems by going into the business of
giving dances. At first they were lovely work, dragging
ice and cases of beer to halls that the Pleasure Committee had rented from sympathetic churches. We would
dance our asses off, tripping on mescaline, the Welcoming Committee cooling our heated faces with fresh
water from a sprayer, surrounding dancing couples with
paper garlands and distributing glittering favors, rings
and things that had a delightful carnival tackiness about
them. We were overcome by our own presence. A single
"vibe" filled the room of writhing bodies. To some eyes
we must have seemed like the end of Western civiliza-
tion, men dancing with men, women with women, our
hair long and damp with sweat, half undressed, our
torsos agleam with changing colored lights, undulating
to the inner-ear penetrations of the rock. We were a
single mass. We celebrated ourselves and our solidarity.

The Pleasure Committee believed we could liberate
our own heads and our sense of community at these
dances, but the political people, believing we were dilut-
ing our purposes, accused the pleasure people of trying
to "dance their way to liberation." We needed our

money and our people for demonstrations, not for decorating dance halls, they maintained. But the money came from the dances, the pleasure people reminded them. The two groups clashed, threatening to tear the fledgling organization apart, holding dramatic late-night meetings to confront each other, beginning to split into two separate camps and to hate each other in the process. They were temporarily bandaged together with an attempt to decorate the dances in political motifs, but an ideological rift had been created, and for some it never healed. In the end the dances proved to be neither political nor pure pleasure. The dances were good business.

But for me they were something else. I was not on the business side of the rainbow. One night, sweeping up after a dance, I encountered a middle-aged black woman sitting somewhat tiredly in the sideline shadows. There were still knots of people lingering about, but she scarcely looked as if she'd come to dance.

"Are you waiting for anyone?" I asked, pushing a broomful of confetti and feeling especially splendid.

"My boy," she said. "He only fourteen, but he already know he's gay, and I'd rather he be here than out in the streets. Here he can meet people, learn about hisself the bess way. But he only fourteen. I don't want him goin' out by hisself, don' you agree? I don' mind him dancin' and all, but he jess a boy. He ain' ready to be goin' home wid strangers. That's what I figure."

"I figure the same." I smiled.

Both our dances and our meetings were filled with the many sorts of people who had come from everywhere to the gay Mecca of New York. We had come in search of protective anonymity, and we had all wound up in the same gigantic closet. Now we were unlocking its door together. WASP mothers back in the Middle West were being told; bankers' bosses and black militants' brothers, ministers' church boards and students' teachers were being told. Most proceeded with some degree of caution, more willing to chance a demonstration and possible arrest than to sit down on the living room couch and look a father in the eye and say, "I am a homosexual." But each time some photographer came to take a picture of a GAA meeting, fewer and fewer people moved out of range. Wherever we came from, whoever we were, we looked with common boldness into the camera's eye.

I was encountering for the first time people I probably would never have encountered elsewhere, people of every political persuasion, from an anarchist who wrote constitutions to a barefoot capitalist who wore a gold dollar sign around his neck. We even had a resident witch. Every local religion was represented and a few imported ones as well, but The Movement superseded them all. The men vastly outnumbered the women, and there were only a few open transvestites and leather sadomasochists and blacks, but there was some representation of almost everyone.

How else could I have met Keith Robertson, my handsome opponent for secretary, who had been the first man to kiss me on the street, and his lover Calvin, whom Keith had met back home in Michigan, but who eventually moved to Amsterdam, where it was easier to be black? How could I have met "Rosa" (Emilio) Garcia, who petitioned for gay rights on Forty-Second Street? "Rosa" was a somewhat bedraggled transvestite who was arrested more often than most of the rest of us put together. "She" wore makeup which was generally heavy—mascara and lipstick that easily smeared—and stockings that were usually torn. But "she" could show up at a dance looking like a Times Square debutante, with a fall of hair almost long enough to reach the hem of the sequined miniskirt he wore with

Cleopatra eyes, until in my mind "he" became a "she," and I referred to him as "her." Rosa had organized STAR (Street Transvestites Action Revolutionaries). It provided communal living quarters on the Lower East Side for her "sisters" in drag. STAR confronted GAA with the needs of the "street people," our own gay kin, who were poor and hungry while we ate in middle-class comfort and guilt. Rosa was waging her own private war.

Rosa, Keith, Calvin, and I stayed awake one night, walking beneath the Brooklyn Bridge and peeing into the East River and playing on the swings in Tomkins Square Park, where by day the elbowroom was shared by hippies and junkies and old Ukrainian ladies. I talked to Rosa as dawn approached, and she told me what it was like to be a hustler in drag in Times Square, and it's not *Midnight Cowboy:* it's being tough enough to pass yourself off as a woman, to use "I got the rag on" as an excuse for only giving blow jobs. She told me what it was like in jail, where sometimes they set gays apart for "protection," where we are the lowest caste, the property of other inmates who are straight and anxious to prove it by the way they molest their ersatz "women," unless those "women" are tough enough. Rosa was tough enough. She didn't have a heart of gold. She bit and scratched and kicked her way through life, with sharp wiles and a gigantic need for love.

It wasn't easy to give it. Everything I had been raised to be was threatened by what Rosa was. Walking down the street with her was more than holding hands with a man who acted pretty much like myself. It was a statement that I considered myself in the same un-privileged class from which my mother had struggled so hard to extract herself. But there was solidarity. And through it I could find behind "Rosa" someone who was once named Emilio Garcia, and if not to applaud his artifice, at least to accept him as a human being.

In spite of the new world of people I was meeting, GAA was already being assailed as a club for white middle-class butch males. The women formed a separate committee. The blacks and Latins formed a separate committee. To my eyes, however, even though volunteers couldn't be attracted in the proper demographic proportions, they could certainly be attracted in enough interesting sorts. We were quite a collection.

There were the maimed among us: the lonely ones, some homely or old, some shy and in need of a friend, the people who were already social outcasts before the question of their being gay ever came up. Some of them weren't even gay at all, only homeless: the hunched woman with shopping bags, the vacant-eyed man with stubbled cheek who drooled after leadership like a promiscuous puppy. Some were gay among their eccentricities, like wearing hat and coat and sunglasses all year round, indoors and out, or wandering Christopher Street at 4 A.M. loudly intoning *a cappella* and clutching a Lucite lunch pail like a purse. The "Trash Committee," an informal group of social commentators, called them "Burie Woman" and "Quasimodo" and "Pocketbook Man." One they called "Snake Man," because he would say at meetings, "We need a snake for the terlit." He was a building superintendent from uptown. He offered us free janitorial service as his contribution to The Movement. "The Tamale of Death" was a Cuban refugee who was always near hysteria, fearing our demonstrations would make us into "Communiss" like the forces of Castro whom he had fled. He would defend his chosen champions in GAA against their opponents with tears, embarrassingly declaring before a bemused meeting of nearly two hundred, "I love Marty Robisson. He is my bess fran!" Marty

hardly knew him. There were those who needed a
home. The Trash Committee labeled them the "trolls,"
but they had their home.

I could watch the rows of faces as I took the minutes
of our meetings from the front of the room. They composed a living mosaic, a single face with constantly
shifting expressions. We were a collection of conform-
ists and individuals no more exotic than any crowd
picked at random from the campuses and offices and
streets of New York City. We called ourselves an army
of lovers, and though most of us were single, many
traveled in pairs or in groups. We practiced all forms
of relating, from compulsive chastity to glad promiscuity and every sexual stripe in between.

Sex was everywhere. With newly eroticized eyes I
looked at firm chests and strong thighs, at the grace of
men walking, the security offered by their arms. Sex
could happen anywhere at any time. I was always ready.
I looked with open admiration at the men I passed in
the street. Sometimes strangers would smile hello, thinking I knew them, or thinking the same thing I was, and
then there was sex, spontaneous and delightful. Sex
with darkly handsome strangers, sex with suddenly attractive friends. My eyes made love to anyone and
anything they touched. My body made love to everyone
it could, proudly offering and receiving pleasure, restrained only by the limits of imagination.

Though sex ran lovely riot through the Gay Activists
Alliance, we were more than an orgy: we were a tribe
with all the complex loves and political rivalries of a
nation. We sent each other lambda Christmas cards.
We jockeyed for power. We argued about love. Love
was an important topic. We loved our lovers. Hearing
that philosophy student Arthur Wallace and gay jour-
nalist Arthur Bell were having domestic difficulty was
like hearing a cousin was ill. One Arthur was reason-

able, the other a romantic, but their characters went together for us like their names: Arthur and Arthur. We worried for their affair of six years. Affairs were important. They were proof that we could do it, proof that we stood for something real.

Our couples included liberated feminists in revolutionary overalls, dedicated to equality with each other and with men. We had a few traditional "butch and femme" pairs, one in pants and one in skirts, who followed the spirit if not the theory of liberation. We also had liberal theoreticians, like Barbara Gittings and Kay Tobin, both in casual slacks. The same was true among the pairs of men. There were quiet traditional couples from New Jersey, in print shirts and penny loafers. There were Marc Rubin and Peter Fisher openly wearing matching leather outfits, sometimes with a flower woven among the chains that proclaimed their sexual tastes. There were the drag queens who spoke of their "husbands."

Marty Robinson's lover then was Tom Doerr, a handsome blond man of wise demeanor. They were the first open lovers to appear on the cover of *Gay*. But the world around was not always as inspired by openly gay affection as I was. It could occasionally be provoked to hostility, even in permissive Greenwich Village. One night, after dinner with Marty and Tom and Jim Owles only a few blocks from home, I kissed Tom lightly good-bye, overhearing a straight teen-ager mutter "Faggots" as he passed.

Marty saw red and pursued the kid with cries of "Punk" until the next corner, where a few of the kid's friends were waiting. Fists and fury flew everywhere, embroiling Marty and Tom and Jim while I stood dumbstruck, surrounded by the melee.

Someone came up to me and asked, "You want some too?"

"No, thanks," I answered, ashamed of the fear that kept me from helping, and ashamed of emerging from the eye of the fracas unscathed, while Marty had a broken nose and Tom had a dislocated jaw. Yet in spite of the lacerations to our pride, all of us were more determined than ever to be open about our love.

It was love of a sort that bound us all together, and we were lovers of every sort. "Little John Basso," as we know John Wojtewicz, wore fringed G-strings to dances and threw us into a quandry about whether it was liberated to host his weddings. While we debated the merits of imitating heterosexual marriage in our relationships, he went on to become the "gay bank robber" in the headlines, his story eventually told in the film *Dog Day Afternoon,* because he tried to finance an operation for his would-be transsexual "bride." And we had a mixed married couple, male and female, who brought a pleasing pansexual tone to our proceedings, experimenting sexually with every combination of people they could devise.

I became part of a couple when I asked Bud to dance after a meeting.

"Ah, the secretary is asking me to dance!" he exclaimed.

"Not the secretary. Just a guy."

We were lovers for several patches of the next year, almost to the point of my moving in. But Bud wasn't free. He was still attached to his family, for whom he worked in their jewelry concern. He was bonded and afraid of losing his legal status. He became the treasurer of GAA in spite of them, and he lived with their disapproval when they found out. I knew that Bud wasn't Mr. Right, but he satisfied me sexually, while I felt guilty for not being able to trade places, tit for tat, when we were in bed and to give as good as I got. But we walked happily hand in hand nonetheless.

The more public we were, the more other lovers cringed in their closets. Our openness threatened them with the disclosure that could end their secret rites, their specialness, and most of all their security. Some of the people we purported to represent were cheering us on from the secrecy of the sidelines, sending anonymous donations and painful letters. Others didn't want us rocking the boat, adding to the public's stereotype of the effete fairy and the diesel dyke a new image: loud demonstrators flaunting our lack of the artful manners they painstakingly hid behind. The left attacked us as reformers, and the right assumed we were rowdies and radicals. The women called us chauvinists. The street queens labeled us bourgeois. We were everything that everyone called us and more. We were a revolution.

In August of 1970, we set out to liberate the oppressed and learned a lesson about violence, surprising the press and the police, but surprising ourselves most of all. It had been over a year since the Stonewall Revolt we so highly vaunted as the beginning of our fighting back. Violence is not without form. Nothing is without form seen from the right perspective. But it can happen without plan or purpose.

Arrests have been heavy on Forty-Second Street. And we are guilty of not relating to the street people, the hustlers and transvestites and terrified out-of-town gays whose sex lives converge in Times Square. People are being arrested on trumped-up charges, hustled in and out of police cars and courts with bored judges, simply to terrorize them. We have always been available victims when the police need a few arrests in order to satisfy the politicians who, usually just before elections, need to impress the public with a "cleanup" of Times Square. There is sentiment in it for me. The Port Authority building which housed my first forays into the gay world is only a block or two away from the heartland of our oppression, though it is miles away from my current life. We decide to declare our solidarity with a world we know little of by staging a demonstration in the middle of the honky-tonk glitter.

About three hundred demonstrators from several gay groups mass at Eighth Avenue and Forty-Second Street, the hastily summoned press interviewing the fringes of our ranks and filling notebooks with our answers to their puzzled inquiries. We raise our posters, our banners, our voices high and march along Forty-Second to Broadway, one long block, and back on the opposite side of the street to where we began, around and around, again and again, chanting our slogans, walking in circles. The hustlers cringe in the doorways, afraid our innocent enthusiasm will pierce their valuable invisibility. With anger in their eyes they finally flee, along with the gays who have come here to be anonymous. And we are abandoned by the oppressed souls we have come to liberate, left to show the tourists what they have come to see in New York, without charging even the admission prices that are advertised beneath the salaciously gaudy movie marquees whose incessantly blinking lights illuminate our faces as we march, hundreds of us, responding to Jim's "Two-four-six-eight . . ." and to Rosa's desperate "Give me a Gee. . . ."

"Gee. . . ."

"Give me an Ayyyy. . . ."

"Ayyyy . . ." until we spell out "Gay Power!"

"I can't hear you: louder."

"Gay Power!"

"When do we want it?"

"Nowww. . . ."

Finally there seems no point to win by circling once more. We have stated our message to the police. After a hasty conference, the leaders of the several groups decide we should leave the scene en masse, our safety as always in our solidarity. We march to the local precinct on what turns out to be a deserted side street, and we move past without stopping to demonstrate, suddenly aware that the silent buildings form a dark canyon in which a "pacification" of our forces could take its bloody course with no notice by the world outside or, worse, with that world's approval.

"Stay together till we get to the Village. Stay together."

"Right on!" We convince ourselves with a trope of the period, and we march the two miles downtown toward Greenwich Village, needing each other, following silent Seventh Avenue, which for all its ominous emptiness is still able to punctuate our rising anxiety with a rock and a bottle tossed from anonymous windows into our nervous midst.

We arrive at the Village to find the Saturday-night tourist throng milling all over Eighth Street, which has been experimentally made into a mall for the summer evening. We are in front of the Women's House of Detention, where people traditionally yell from the sidewalk, "Maria, the lawyer says . . ." and someone among us cries out, "Free our sisters! Free ourselves!" Following Jim's instructions the GAA banner is folded. Our constitution pledges us to nonviolence and support of only gay causes, and this is clearly an incendiary moment. Most of us stay, some turning their lambda T-shirts inside out in deference to the constitution, most ready to explode, along with the rest of the crowd, which for its own reasons surges toward us from Eighth Street as if on cue, and suddenly we are all one mob of thousands. Again we chant, "Free our sisters," and the incarcerated women, hearing, begin to throw burning papers from their cell windows in solidarity. They become revolutionary streamers in the darkness, and it feels as if we are before the Bastille in another time and place.

When the surge of the crowd takes us the few blocks to Sheridan Square, we find what we fear. The police and the firemen are mutually harassing The Haven, a loud, all-night juice bar, where the drug freaks dance past dawn with the hearty disapproval of the neighbors. Some of them are gay, and we see it as an affront to the very demonstration we have just come from, as fists begin to pound on cars in a fury that is helplessly contagious, until we are chanting gay liberation/peace movement words: "Two-four-six-eight; We don't want a fascist state," and suddenly they are upon us, a flying wedge of bluecoats who mean business, nothing like the friendly cop who took me across the street to Maple Avenue School in Newark with white-gloved hands. Clubs are flying, heads, elbows everywhere, feet running, people clustering and scrurrying back to the House of Detention, back to Sheridan Square, faces of friends fleeing, frantic strangers being bloodied to the ground with nightsticks, shirts ripped, bones stomped and broken, bottles thrown from the back of the crowd, pressing us forward into chaos.

Can these be the streets where I live? The stores where I buy my milk and bread? The sound of breaking glass clattering. Screams in the night. Epithets of hatred and pain. Everything is upside down until we are exhausted. And almost miraculously I am three blocks from home having an ice cream soda with Arthur Wallace and Arthur Bell, mumbling in amazement, "Only in America can we rest from revolution with butter pecan."

It was too dangerous to pass through Sheridan Square to get the Sunday *Times* on my way home. The sound of tinkling glass punctuated the breathless air: night-sticks breaking bottles that might become weapons. For hours the crowd ran amok, overturning cars, trashing shops through broken windows, setting fires. It was a taste of chaos, and I didn't much like it. It had no purpose, not even revolt. All that everyone had in common was the hot August night and the romance of revolution, the legacy of Che Guevara. I learned that night that insurrection is more fun in Technicolor than it is around the corner.

I woke on Sunday morning not knowing what I would find outside my very door at ground zero. There were boarded windows, broken glass, a Volkswagen on its side, but the streets showed no lasting scars. A thousand separate reasons for human frustrations to burst were swept up together with the morning's refuse, only to be forgotten. In the early sunlight it was as if it had never happened at all. Perhaps a bad dream. Perhaps the darker side of Oz.

We fellow travelers to gay liberation shared the special kind of bond that outcasts share. Each of us had made an arduous journey, and as different as we were in lifestyle, we needed each other as exiles from the same country do. GAA quickly became a world of our own, with our own laws and leaders, our own idols, and our own enemies to zap. Zapping always made me feel like a guerrilla making forays into straight territory. It was more thrilling than the movies. We took over the offices of *Harper's* magazine for a day to protest an article they had published in which we were wished off the face of the earth, and to reeducate them over coffee and doughnuts. That same day we went on to infiltrate the lines of "The Dick Cavett Show," planning to disrupt the video-taping with whistles. Before we could do our number, they found out and negotiated with us until Marty Robinson and

Arthur Wallace ended up telling our side of things on television. We picketed Fidelifacts, an organization that told prospective employers we were gay. The owner had remarked on how he decided whether someone actually was gay: "If it looks like a duck and talks like a duck, and if it hangs out with other ducks, it probably is a duck." Marty got into a rented duck outfit for the picket line and quacked us on as we rushed upstairs to confront the oppressor in his lair, disrupting his file cabinets in the uproar.

Arthur Wallace knew that it was easy to disrupt an office merely with a display of the wrong manners. One day the target was Household Finance, for refusing loans to known gays. We leaped from branch office to branch office like midtown Manhattan gazelles, surprising them in one after the other. Arthur confronted the managers in a suddenly angry voice: "Are you proud of yourself, mister? Are you proud that homosexuals can't get a loan here? Answer me!" And the rest of us chorused, "Answer the homosexual!" to their bewildered ears. It felt like nothing could stop us.

But we weren't only zapping. We also worked within the system. Jim and I went to visit Councilman Eldon Clingan to propose that "sexual orientation" be added to all antidiscrimination statutes in the city. We wanted a fair employment law for gays. We devoted a whole committee to passage of our bill, which was called Intro 475. GAA had undertaken enough projects to require nearly two dozen committees, to the point where we needed a Committee on Committees just to sort them out. By the time they were restructured, most of them had already given birth to subcommittees. Subcommittees generated forms to fill out, red tape to cut through, complications. We were developing into a bureaucracy before our own eyes.

Bureaucracy was only one of the issues as we headed

into our elections at the end of 1970. We were at odds in several arenas, and as December grew near, the campaign began to heat our discussions. Accusation and suspicion flew thick as the race took shape. Jim wanted to stay in office. Aaron Lloyd wanted to unseat him, murmuring fire about Jim's morals, manners, and politics. Aaron stood for internal self-liberation. He was chairman of the Police Power Committee. Arthur Wallace was in the race, and his lover, Arthur Bell, openly defying him, supported Aaron. And Cary Yurman was in the race simply to speak his own piece. The whole thing was of secondary interest for me. I was running for the vice-presidency.

My opponent was Pete Fisher, a popular hero who had organized the zap of *Harper's* magazine. Compared to the furor over the presidency, which had spread to the gay community at large, our campaign seemed gentlemanly. Our statements on the floor of general meetings were not opposed. We liked each other and wished each other well. Everything would depend on the presentations we made on nominations night. I asked my friend Vito to nominate me. He was a good choice: everybody liked Vito, and he could speak well. But just to be certain I wrote the nominating speech myself.

I arrived at the meeting rehearsing my acceptance in my head. It was a plea for solidarity of national scope to be delivered in the manner of Golda Meir. The meeting hall in back of the church was packed as tight as the most popular bar of the season on a Saturday night. Hundreds of curious gay people had come to see the circus. I was nervously readying my speech while the show opened.

Helen MacNulty, the leader of the GAA softball team, nominated Aaron Lloyd with the bombshell declaration that Jim had been Marty Robinson's puppet throughout his administration. Ears perked right up.

Aaron accepted the nomination gently, claiming to seek only freedom from Jim's tyranny. He was nicked from the right during the question period when someone in back hurled, "Weren't you a member of SDS?" It caused a flutter in the audience, but it was an obvious tactic by one of his opponents to complicate things. Aaron denied it.

Arthur Wallace—quietly, it seemed—sought a redefinition of the presidency, speaking of the potential for organizing a national movement. Arthur Bell in a tuxedo, fresh from a theater opening, sat across the room with Holly Woodlawn, a transvestite star in the Andy Warhol firmament, whom he had brought for the occasion.

Cary Yurman accepted his nomination with evident integrity. He didn't really expect to win, but he wanted to use the nomination as a forum in order to draw our attention to his views. Aaron was all right, he guessed. He would probably vote for Aaron. Jim, as we all knew, was Marty Robinson's puppet. But did we know that Arthur Wallace was an anarchist bent on using gay liberation as a tool in his schemes of violence? All we had to do was ask his lover, Arthur Bell. He knew.

Arthur Wallace jumped to his feet and thundered, "And isn't it true that you've been sleeping with my lover for the last three months?"

The audience gasped as one. This was the sexual politics everyone had come to see! A buzz stirred the room as Arthur Bell made his way to the front, denying everything. "Cary is only my friend. You're trying to exploit us all!" Arthur accused Arthur of Machiavellian plots in a tirade of personal pain, and the rest of us sat captive audience to the list of grievances until it was publicly certified that Arthur and Arthur had reached an end. So had the childhood of the Gay Activists Alliance, and so had my political naïveté.

In the furor that followed, Jim and I were nominated. A week later he was reelected president, and I was elected to the vice-presidency. I was exhilarated and sobered both. I had just had a hell of a year, and an even more promising one lay ahead.

8

LIFE WAS A PERPETUAL CRISIS, AND I LOVED IT. IT
was the most political year in my experience. The battle
for progressive education occupied my days, and the
power struggles of gay liberation usurped my nights.
Some days, between the educators and the activists,
I sat through four or five meetings, whose tense con-
frontations frequently bordered on physical violence.
At school we assailed the leadership; in GAA we protected it. The dialogues were so nearly the same, save
for whether I was on the offense or the defense, that
I had to keep track of my surroundings, or I was afraid
I'd end up arguing on the wrong side in the wrong
arena. I saw everything with politician's eyes that year.
I suspected wily motives in everyone and planned
Byzantine maneuvers to deal with them. It made everything self-conscious, including the sex life I scarcely
had time to conduct. I was so busy getting liberated
that there was hardly any time left to be gay. Luckily,
the gay world keeps very late hours, so merely by
cutting down on my sleep I was able to juggle education
and politics and sex with reasonable dexterity.

As the vice-president I could cruise Christopher Street not only with confidence but with a little strut. There is a public decorum that goes with any elected office, and mine required me to greet a hundred people as I promenaded back and forth looking for sex. It got so friendly that it became difficult to cruise. My self-confidence was shored up by having a constituency in GAA, and I felt more attractive, if not utterly secure in my appearance, having lost the pounds that frustration had piled on my frame. So when enough people suggested that I try the baths, I was willing to take the risk of being seen in public in a towel in order to find sexual paradise. I began at a pleasure palace called The Continental, and I liked it enough to become a steady customer for the next two years.

The baths were where to act out dreams. The hallways formed a circuitous maze whose air was thick with dim red light. The only hints of a world outside were through scratches in the black paint that coated the window at the end of a third-floor corridor. It was always night at the baths, protected from the reality outside the door by a thick layer of gay imagination that sealed us in a secure environment as if we were in a huge magic theater where we could forget for a few hours what society thought of us.

The corridors were lined with metal doors, occasionally open, revealing a small cubicle with a sponge mattress on a narrow ledge. The men inside toyed with their cocks invitingly, waiting in an amazing variety of poses in the dimness: standing, sitting on the edges of beds, pinching their nipples submissively, suggestively spreading their knees, or lying on their bellies, asses up, hoping to be fucked. Everything was perfectly blatant. There was no need for shame: we were all wrapped in similar towels, all seeking our own personal versions of the same thing. Any hint would do to build a fantasy on: an eye patch or a pair of boots incongruously worn with the towel, an artfully shaded light bulb, a spread of sadomasochist's "toys," a ribbon. All were worn unabashedly. In our towels we could be sleeping with anyone, a garbageman or an astronaut, and never know the difference.

It was simply a matter of asking for sex by entering a room after lingering in the doorway long enough to exchange looks in the dimness, long enough for me to imagine a childhood pirate or Heathcliff holding me in his arms, Rhett Butler smiling knowingly, or Mr. Right. With my stock of images I had sexual contact with a dozen men in a night. We spoke with our bodies first. I let my affection feel its way, offering it freely to men I didn't know, making love to them for their generic maleness because individual personalities couldn't be seen, unless we chose to reveal them later. I let my masochist's fantasies emerge, relieved to play them out unashamed, calling strangers "sir," or even "Daddy," and growing freer with each part of myself that I faced, helped to orgasm by a brotherhood of loyal strangers.

It wasn't total anonymity. There were exploratory conversations after orgasm, while the heady smell of the amyl nitrite "poppers" we used as aphrodisiacs still lingered in the air. Occasionally there were exchanges of phone numbers, sometimes leading to dates. Or there was simply a heartfelt "Thanks," or a polite excuse like "I have to take a shower," and then farewell. It was as personal as we chose to make it.

The dormitory was popularly known as the "orgy room." At first I was afraid to go in, but eventually I tried it. I went a little deeper into its shadows each time. The third time I went, I stayed for the better part of a night in the pitch darkness of its mattressed recesses, filled with anonymous touches of men, surrounded by total flesh, total humanity, reveling in

grunts and sighs and slurps and sudden farts and
laughter, sharing saliva with lips I never saw, swallowing strange semen. I kept falling asleep like a puppy in
a litter only to be awakened by somebody rolling over
and brushing against me, to have sex with him and go
back to sleep only to be roused by somebody from the
other side and have sex with him. It was the freedom
of facelessness. It was pure flesh, fucking until I was
no longer sure where I ended and the already forgotten
count of men began. It went on for hours until suddenly
I felt engulfed, as if I were drowning in flesh all around
me, behind me, inside me, uncontrollably. I had lost
charge of my own body! I was nothing but orfice. I
grew desperate; I had to escape. There was no time
to be polite, no time to explain. I pushed the body
behind me unceremoniously away. He grabbed at me,
uncertain in the darkness what was happening, wanting
to finish. I was in a sea of arms and legs and stiffened
cocks. I felt smothered as if by quicksand, as if I were
falling asleep, and I realized with a panic that unless
I used all my energy to awaken, I might lose my own
body and die. I fled from the room like a swimmer
bursting from beneath the surface of a pool when
someone's held his head under for a moment too long,
in one long burst through the waves of men to the
doorway, desperate for air. The red-lit hall was a
relief. Looking down at myself to see if I were in fact
in my own skin, I discovered I was standing foolishly
naked, my towel clutched in my hand. I wrapped it
around me and headed for the shower, ready to split
from paradise for the night.

I never ventured far past the edges of the orgy room
after that, but I remained an advocate of intimacy,
continuing my affair with promiscuity, only adding a
lot more discretion and some light. I liked the baths.
Even when I was with strangers. I could offer human

love, and when love was there, we weren't quite strangers anymore, at least if I could help it.

On Saturday nights there was a stage show open to the public. New entertainers like Bette Midler would sing to an audience of us in our towels and a growing cabaret crowd in their street clothes. It was fun at first, a camp. But as the months went on, the word spread, and the crowd grew huge. It was the "in" place to be, written up in all the columns as the latest word in chic decadence. Weimar Republic modern. And I was the decor! I sat next to women who tried not to notice my carelessly draped towel, wondering if I should get dressed or expose myself and get it over with. I watched men in suits watch me nervously as I danced, wanting to go up and introduce myself as an Assistant Professor of English. Eventually I felt like a trained bear in a zoo. If I was the attraction, how come I was paying admission? Saddened, I took my trade elsewhere. We had struggled to become visible, and our very visibility was inviting people to come to see us, to threaten inadvertently with their presence the edges of our private world, making us feel "different" in our own territory because they were wearing clothes, and we were naked.

I had learned to relish feeling different in public and to make my difference manifest in whatever ways I could. Putting clothes on didn't do a lot to make me inconspicuous. I was wearing my long hair with a bushy set of red mutton-chop whiskers meeting my moustache. My orange eyeglasses and my jewelry went well with my studded pants, I thought, but when I went to see my mother, she didn't agree at all.

She and Frank were trying to recoup at least a modest part of their losses by running a small luncheonette in Jersey City, an endeavor that lasted only several months before bankruptcy. There was a bitterness I could see about her as I entered the yellow and green, Formica-linoleum-chrome jukebox of a room. This was not the life she had ordered. She still wanted Scarlett O'Hara's mansion in Atlanta. I could see it in her eyes as I dutifully bent to kiss her cheek.

She recoiled before I could reach it. "Feh," she said. "So much hair. It's disgusting." I stayed the afternoon, but that was the last time I visited her. I had better things to do.

GAA had acquired a home of its own, and it kept us all busy. It was an engine company building which had been abandoned by the Fire Department years before, tucked into Wooster Street in the artists' loft neighborhood of SoHo, just around the corner from Supernova, where I had worked at educational experiment only two years before. We called our new home The Firehouse. The ten-minute walk between it and Christopher Street became very familiar ground to a host of gay feet in the following months.

The basement held committee meetings. The first floor, where the engines had been stored, was lined with white tile. It made a good hall for general membership meetings. A small spiral stairway led to the second floor, which was used for a snack bar, informal sitting around, and more committee meetings. The top floor was for offices and, of course, still more committee meetings. There was no shortage of meetings. There were so many meetings that, in spite of all the room, space had to be booked in advance.

At the dedication ceremonies in May, 1971, I stood on the spiral staircase and pointed at the new mural that stretched across the tile wall on the first floor in a series of photomontage panels. The audience was composed of friends and those politicians who had begun to take us seriously, like the head of the General Welfare Committee of New York's City Council, where our fair employment and housing bill, Intro 475, was already gathering dust, waiting for the committee to meet. I don't know what the mural seemed to him, but to me it was a family portrait. It was the way we saw ourselves: a homosexual clutching iron bars in anguish (cropped from a picture that revealed the bars to belong to the fence in a public park), Walt Whitman and Gertrude Stein and black militant Huey Newton endorsing our cause, Jim Owles at City Hall, Vito Russo in Albany, Allen Ginsberg, men embracing, women holding hands, slogans such as GAY POWER, GAY PRIDE, AN ARMY OF LOVERS CANNOT LOSE, my erstwhile lover Bud and I holding hands in the streets of Washington, D.C. The mural was something for homosexuals to be proud of.

But when most of them came to The Firehouse on Saturday nights, it couldn't be seen. The meeting hall became a dance floor packed with a shoulder-to-shoulder sea of dancers undulating to the deafening blast of soul rock, an awesome sight from halfway up the spiral staircase, which was perpetually too crowded to afford more than a hasty glimpse of all that rhythmic homosexuality. Some fifteen hundred or so people passed through on an average Saturday night. GAA tried to seduce some of them to the third floor to watch videotapes of our political zaps, but they had come to dance. And the mural hung unnoticed by them, a vague backdrop obscured in the flashing of stroboscopic lights. As far as most of the dancers knew, they were in the hottest bar in town. The political people were none too happy with this state of affairs, but in spite of it some optimist scrawled in the basement, "Avenge Sodom and Gomorrah," and the struggle continued.

Our next step in trying to pass Intro 475 was to convince Thomas Cuite, the majority leader of the City Council, to schedule the hearings. Cuite wouldn't even give us an appointment to discuss it, so we found ourselves at the steps of City Hall demanding to be heard. A dozen gays infiltrated the building, a few of them chaining themselves to desks in public protest. Fifty or so of us remained outside, at first pretending to picket, then laying siege to City Hall, trying to enter or to be publicly prevented in order to draw attention to the Second Annual Christopher Street Liberation Day parade, which was to be the following Sunday. We were holding street fairs, dancing gaily in the streets before The Firehouse, scheduling cabarets where singers wouldn't have to change the pronouns in their songs, and exhibiting agitprop to raise community consciousness. We called it Gay Pride Week. Our solidarity was running high, and the action at City Hall was timed to bring our political struggle to the public's awareness.

As we attempted to enter the front door of the city's municipal center, police tried to disperse us. People were running everywhere. Jim and I sat down on the top step only to have our grips ripped forcibly from the banister by unyielding policemen's hands. They flung us rudely to the bottom of the stair, but we managed to keep on our feet. Jim immediately charged again. He was caught and taken off to be arrested. I turned to run from a mounted policeman whose horse pawed at my heels insistently, just behind me, no matter which way I ran, until I reached safety behind a parked car.

I had little time to catch my breath before I found another policeman in front of me, demanding, "Move, or you'll be put under arrest."

"What are we doing that's illegal?" asked a voice next to me. It was Vito's lover, the secretary of GAA.

"Just move, or you'll be put under arrest."

We stood our ground with solidarity. The next thing

we knew, we were being led into the recesses of City Hall.

Almost as soon as we crossed the threshold into the dimness of the corridor, the fury seemed to have been left outside in the sunlight. We were led to a small room. A total of nine of us had been arrested—"the Cuite Nine," GAA dubbed us. My hands were cuffed behind my back. But we were treated decently, like demonstrators, not molested or even insulted as "fags," in spite of the many tales I had heard of beatings and rapes in police-station basements. It was as if there had been a play going on outside, and once backstage we could all of us drop our masks. They turned out our pockets and herded us into the paddy wagon, where we comforted ourselves with wisecracks in the dark heat, emboldened by our polite reception.

Seven hours with my hands cuffed behind me in the Fifth Precinct station house is not my idea of a pleasant afternoon. One by one we were led aside to be photographed by the Red Squad. Red Squad? I thought. I'm saying cocksucking, and they're hearing communism.

For hours I waited to be processed, silently watching the life in the station house go by, young rookies self-consciously squaring their shoulders as they passed the place where the older cops were sitting. Being butch is as much of an artifice in a police station as it is in a gay bar, and a good deal less promising. I was bored. Finally my arresting officer turned to me.

"The object of these questions is to build enough points to let you out on a Vera Summons."

"What's a Vera Summons?"

"On your own recognizance. Got it?"

I nodded.

"Name?"

"Kantrowitz."

"Spell it."

"K-A-N, T-R-O—"

"Wait a minute. Not so fast. Was that T-O-R?" He struggled with the form, a stranger to the written language. I could have filled it out in a few minutes, but he took closer to half an hour.

"How long have you resided at the same address?"

"Five years."

"Do any members of your family reside in the greater metropolitan area?"

"My family lives in New Jersey."

"How many times a year do you see them?"

"Uh, three or four." I stretched it.

"How long have you been at your present employment?"

I calculated quickly. "Six years."

"You'll have no problem getting a Vera," he said encouragingly.

"Wait'll you hear what I do." I relaxed immediately.

He returned to his form. "Where are you employed?"

"Staten Island Community College."

He looked up at me. "Yeah? Are you a professor?"

"Assistant Professor."

"What subject do you teach?"

"English."

"Oh yeah?" he warmed. "You know, I live on Staten Island. In fact I was thinking of taking a course at Community . . . English in fact."

"Mm-hmm," I encouraged.

"A night course," he continued. "Do you teach night school? Listen, I'll make a deal with you. Say I sign up for one of your courses. If I pass you on this Vera, will you pass me on the exam?" He chuckled with his own cleverness.

"Sure," I said. "By the way, what's your name?"

"Francis," he said, and then he added, looking

hastily around, "Frank, the guys all call me Frank."
He smiled.

I still say hello to Frank whenever I'm down at
City Hall.

The following Sunday I marched proudly up Sixth
Avenue in our second gay liberation parade, but something was missing in the march. Nothing could be like
the first time. There were as many people, perhaps
more, but it was only the memory of the mood of a
year earlier that moved me. The rest was speeches I
had heard before.

I left for the beach right after the march. It was a
chance to see the fabled Fire Island and to share a
house with seven other men from GAA. Living in a
group provided constant company. It drew me to the
island more and more. I started with weekends, but
they grew longer and longer until I returned to the
city only for Executive Committee and general membership meetings. I had been enchanted. If ever a
place was over the rainbow, it was Cherry Grove. I
felt as if I were living in a pop-up picture book, a town
over 90 percent gay, filled with dollhouses trimmed to
the eaves in charming gingerbread, pastel paints,
flowered trash cans, geraniums planted in leather
boots, rose hips running wild, gardens profuse with
black-eyed Susans, tiger lilies, sunflowers, daisies, petu-
nias, and no-nonsense pansies. Plus they sold flowers
down by the dock, the first thing to greet new arrivals
as they disembarked from the ferry that had brought
them from the mainland to this fantasia. Cherry Grove
is cute. If you turned it upside down and back, it
would probably snow. The houses had names instead
of numbers: a purple one called "Catherine the Grape,"
a sign spelled in studs on black leather reading "Spank
You Very Much," a lesbian's eyrie called "No Boys
in the Attic," sex and social conscience in "The Pillows

of Society" and "Wounded Knees." We painted our
politics on a piece of driftwood and called our house
"Gay and Proud." For all its store-bought charm,
Cherry Grove was less pretentious than its neighboring
town, The Fire Island Pines, only half as gay but twice
as discreet about it. The Grove crowd was older, less
sophisticated, the crowd from The Pines more fashionable, but they met democratically in the sand-path
shadows that crisscrossed the woods between the
towns. We called the woods the "meat rack." But it
was hard to feel sordid about the sex we had in those
woods, especially when we looked up at the clarity of
stars or caught the hush of the waves from behind the
dunes. It was easier to feel like Sherwood Forest's
Merry Men, full of our own innocence and laughing
at the law. It was a good place to avoid asking where
my politics were taking me. It was as far away from
the Fifth Precinct station house as I could get.

Where the trail takes the first right-angle turn into
the woods from the Grove, there ought to be a com-
memorative plaque saying, "Here, Arnie Kantrowitz,
by the grace of God thirty years of age, first fucked
another man." It happened quickly, a sudden shift of
position in the dark that took me by surprise with its
pleasure. I liked it, but it was still too anonymous for
me.

Cherry Grove is the ideal place for a summer
romance, but no place is totally safe for homosexuals.
One night, nuzzling a date while waiting for a beach
taxi to The Pines, I was confronted by a stranger waiting with his wife and another couple inside the cab:
"Look at them kissing like that! You like kissing your
girl like that?"

It was a voice from another world breaking into the
fragile fantasy that offers a protective envelope to the
town, breaking the Shangri-La spell inside which I

could be "normal," one of the few places in the world where I could be in the majority. "This isn't my girl, it's my guy," I answered. "This is Cherry Grove, remember?"

He sputtered, sounding drunk. "Your guy? That's disgusting. You can't do that in front of me. There are ladies. . . ."

"Shut up, Johnny," his wife said.

Leaning out of the taxi's window, he slapped me on the face.

I slapped him right back. His friends restrained him.

"You don't own this planet," I accused. "We live here too, and we have a right to live our lives the way we want."

In the city I dealt as little as possible with the straight world I passed through, feeling as if I lived in a different dimension, as if I were altogether invisible, simple because my sexual orientation didn't show. I concentrated on the gay world, centering my attention on The Firehouse. From its inception The Firehouse shanghaied our concern away from both the politics and the dances and focused our debates on finance: the management of the property, appropriating money for maintenance, salaries for staff workers and office help, raising the price of "suggested donations" at dances, sales of lambda T-shirts and lambda key chains and lambda shoulder bags, locks to secure the places where our new acquisitions were held—videotape camera, movie projectors, mimeograph, and such—which were stolen in spite of the locks. The treasurer's reports grew longer and longer. We spoke less and less about gay liberation. We grew more and more like the system we were trying to change.

I got a taste of the system when the results of our fracas at City Hall led me to trial. I was glad to rely totally on GAA's solidarity, knowing little of the courts. All I knew was that I wasn't anxious to go to jail, especially after Rosa's vivid descriptions of gay life behind bars. The charges were minor: disorderly conduct for everyone plus a resisting-arrest charge against Jim; yet it took a whole day of testimony and photographs and offers of plea bargaining before we were through. I never even got to testify, but it was just as well. The courtroom was nothing like Hollywood's version of jurisprudence. Most of the action occurred in huddles before the judge's bench. Witnesses were questioned summarily: no cross-examinations, no dramatic revelations, only a good deal of blather about which way who was running when photographed and whether the arrests were in order. I felt like protesting at the waste of my taxpayer's money, but I didn't think it would help my case any. When the day was over, all of us were found not guilty, except for Jim, who was found guilty of disorderly conduct, the lesser of the charges against him. He was dismissed with a warning, evidently the judge's idea of setting an example. At future demonstrations we raised our fists in time with steady chants of "Justice! Justice! Justice!"

GAA administered its own justice rather than rely on the court's. When my sometime lover, Bud, the organization's second treasurer, tried to tally the first year's receipts, which he had inherited from his predecessor, he discovered what looked like evidence of embezzlement. The secret spread through the hierarchy like an energetic staphylococcus at an orgy. It couldn't be ignored; it couldn't be contained. It had to be treated. We brought to bear all of Robert's rules for such a situation and proceeded to stage our own trial, a little more graceful than a kangaroo court, but no worse than the state's justice. As the vice-president I got to be the prosecuting attorney, for which I had little taste after watching the real thing. Following the most elaborate trial we could produce, the culprit was found guilty of some of the charges against him and sentenced to restricted voting and membership privileges. No one wanted revenge. We were satisfied with just enough justice to exonerate the organization's financial name. I had foolishly thought there was no one among us who would take advantage of our naïve idealism, but I was quickly learning otherwise. Not everyone was as idealistic as I. It got so that there were so many fingers in the till there was hardly any room for the money. If "solidarity" was a word of the times, so was "rip-off."

One hot night we gathered in our customary hundreds for our weekly meeting, embroiled in some sober business, our shirts shed, the doors flung wide to welcome any movement of the syrupy, stagnant air on which our rhetoric floated with effort. In the middle of a debate, a hush began to settle on the crowd. One of our members was led in slowly, enfeebled, leaning on a friend's arm. I didn't know him too well. The organization had been growing wildly, and there were new faces all the time. The vice-presidency left me little time to welcome newcomers: we had a committee for that. Whispers preceeded him to the front of the floor, funereal whispers of doom. A pall fell over the assembly. A hastily huddled council met at the podium to ask the meeting to vote to suspend the business at hand to hear from a gay brother who had no time to wait. Nervously, curiously, sentimentally, we voted to suspend.

He was helped to a chair, the microphone lowered to his trembling chin. The hundreds were silent, expectant, awed by the moment of pure theater. His words were as thick as the crowded heat in the room, his phrases slurred so that we had to strain to hear each word. "My brothers and sisters," he worked at saying. Someone turned off the loudly useless fan. "My brothers and sisters: this is . . . last meeting. My last . . . meeting. Tomorrow, I . . . the hospital . . . third operation . . . cancer. Not expected to live. Before I face . . . you to know . . . you have changed my life . . . believe in myself . . . never before. Even if . . . I have felt love from all my . . . beautiful . . . here. Pain so great . . . but had to come . . . farewell . . . thank you . . . love . . . all of you."

We could see each other beginning to weep, struggling with the awkwardness of feeling a dying man's gratitude, knowing that the same was true of our own lives if we were to die that day, knowing that our love for each other, our common struggle—even our struggle with each other—had already been worthwhile, regardless of results in courtrooms and legislative chambers, knowing that each of us belonged to all of us forever, each of us stronger, prouder, more courageous for the solidarity we had shared. Our love, we felt, would transcend even death. There wasn't a dry eye in the house.

The next day we discovered he wasn't dying at all. He didn't even have cancer. He was a down freak who gobbled barbiturates like bonbons. They slurred his speech and stirred his fancy. We never saw him again. He had absconded with the money we had been stowing a dime at a time for months to buy a piano.

But our love and our dreams were not destroyed, only a little weathered by such experiences. When I heard that a group of members were thinking of starting a gay commune, I approached them enthusiastically, anxious to end my years of living alone in my "2½ rms" on Bleecker Street that had long since grown overcrowded with unread books and too much oak furniture and a clutter of cats. The other members of the group were Joe Murray, who worked in a bank, Dave Doyle, an English teacher, Alan Gottlieb, who was reorganizing his life after terminating his marriage, and Larry Nicholson, a bartender ten years younger than the rest of the group.

We found a house on Spring Street, only two blocks from The Firehouse in the northern reaches of Little Italy, where every night at suppertime we could hear perhaps thirty mothers calling "Anthonyyyyy." Moderns called the area the western edge of SoHo, where the local artists came out from their lofts only after the Italian population had gone to sleep. But for us it was the southern extension of Greenwich Village, only ten minutes from Christopher Street, which trip we made as often as we heard its siren call in our loins.

The house had been built in 1792 and had enough charms to inspire a ghost story from a visiting friend who was feeling psychic. Ghosts turned out to be far less of a problem than the faulty plumbing and electricity, which went a long way toward limiting the charm in our eyes. Nonetheless, we loved it, and though we traded rooms and roommates more than once, we felt at home from the first. The kitchen boasted a fireplace and a view of the backyard. Everyone who ate in it remarked on the homey atmosphere of rural hearth that prevailed when we gathered around the long table for dinner. Each of us cooked once a week for the whole group, and weekends were left to potluck. The cleaning was left to goodwill and inspiration and occasional chiding. Somehow or other, the system worked.

The relationships of the men in the house on Spring Street were complex and rich. When they became too rich, when anger or stubborn silence or anarchy threatened the household, we gathered for a house meeting to air our grievances—whether it was unrequited love involving two individuals or hostility between the group and one of its members—and to share our relief when the spirit of calm had been restored. The meetings were our own mixture of group therapy and confrontation politics, inherited from the Sixties, and they worked well, but not well enough to keep us all together permanently.

The house never seemed to have a totally stable population from month to month, with one or another of us taking a lover for a period, and comings and goings predictable only in their suddenness, but in spite of our instability, a family spirit prevailed throughout our stay. Sometimes we were five, sometimes four or six or eight. Along with guests, when we sat down to dinner, we were often ten or more. But always we were a family without benefit of blood tie, with only goodwill to hold us together. We were brothers to each other, fathers and sons to each other, friends and occasional lovers of each other, and for whatever fights we may have had, there were wonderful memories of birthday parties with cakes made by young Larry with too much icing and a precarious tilt and much love, or ordered from a bakery with explicit instructions to word the top, "A *Gay* Twenty-First Birthday," while the baker kept insisting we must mean *"Happy."* But we didn't let bakers and the rest of society bother us. We had set up our own world with its own rules and its own values, and the less we had to do with the world outside our threshold, the better it seemed for us.

We had no shortage of human contact. Aside from each other, we found ample variety in the visitors who came passing through in an endless stream, curious about the way of life we had established. We gave huge parties filling our four stories with our own friends and the friends they brought with them, reaching 150 guests at a time, gay and straight, male and female, everywhere. For hours the floors, the beds, the hallways would be filled wth people, until the crowd thinned out toward dawn and the serious partying could begin, turning the

entire establishment into a four-tiered orgy until well
toward the next noon, or beginning with a quiet holiday
dinner for twenty and lasting through a whole weekend
with so many arrivals and departures that everyone
lost track, and no one had any idea whose guest was
whose, if it had ever mattered in the first place.

We had less and less need of our relatives. We had
each other and our friends. And after a while just each
other seemed enough. The parties began to thin out,
tired of themselves, and we were left more and more
to our own devices, more and more to a world of our
own making. What we had in common was being gay,
and being gay became the focus of our existence. It
dominated our conversations and drove out almost all
other subjects. If our gay consciousness had been raised
high in GAA, it rose altogether out of sight in the house
on Spring Street. It was like living in Never-never Land,
leaving reality far, far below.

But New York's reality remained to be dealt with.
Intro 475 would not pass itself. The political people
of GAA needed to show City Hall that a gay community
did indeed exist. The dancers at The Firehouse didn't
much like their Saturday nights interrupted with dry
political announcements, but the politicos had a better
idea. They could turn a dance into a new adventure
and accomplish their civic mission with the same stroke.
So it was that at two-thirty one Sunday morning, many
hundreds of homosexuals left The Firehouse for the
doormanned apartment building where City Councilman Saul Sharison lived, to tell his neighbors what we
thought of him for not arranging public hearings so
that our bill could be voted out of his committee and
onto the floor of the Council. We stormed the building's lobby, filling the entire block in front of it with
loud chanting and public camping and a platoon of
policemen armed with clubs which they didn't hesi-

tate to use on the stragglers they caught around a dark corner, separated from the rest of the crowd. We woke the entire neighborhood with our anger. Our leaflets informed the local citizenry that Councilman Sharison received an annual extra fee of several thousand dollars for heading the General Welfare Committee, which hadn't even met for well over a year. Within three weeks the first public hearings on civil rights for homosexuals in New York City were under way.

It was a circus. The General Welfare Committee and the Gay Activists Alliance were as good as Barnum and Bailey at putting on a show. The rights of all citizens to housing and employment were obscured by a series of religionists calling down the wrath of Jehovah and/or the Holy Ghost, and the quiet voices of rabbis and priests who spoke of human compassion were drowned. The police and firemen evoked images of anarchy and a city in flames if openly gay men were allowed to patrol the streets or fight fires. The transvestites among us appeared in drag to dramatize their exclusion from the bill's coverage and demanded access to the ladies' room, much to the horror of those council members who believed men were born to wear pants. Women and men offered testimony to prove the discrimination they had suffered in looking for jobs and apartments, but the committee could hear only the housewife from Queens who demanded of the assembly, "Where are your mothers? Is this what we want for our children?" Jim fumed. Vito wept. I sat quietly crocheting a scarf I was learning to make, wondering about the meaning of the motto that decorated the ceiling of the Council chambers: "Equal and exact justice to all men [sic] of whatever state or persuasion." The committee promised its verdict soon.

The next day my brother called. "It's bad enough you have to knit," he demanded, "but do you have to do it on television?" The news of the day was that men crochet.

The leadership of GAA was growing exhausted. The City Council had contempt for us. The dissidents disagreed with us. The transvestites made demands of us. The women and blacks were angry at us. The membership expected the impossible of us. I was beginning to look forward to the end of my term, anxious to tell all factions what I thought of them. On the floor of meetings I insisted time and again that liberation meant not being led, but doing it for yourself. Everyone was too busy squabbling to listen. The top of our hierarchy grew more and more distant from its base, more and more aloof out of self-protection and weariness.

One evening the officers gathered to forget all these woes and to socialize. Politics was forbidden conversation for one night. We ate dinner at a friend's house, and in spite of the fact that no one had been left in command at The Firehouse, we all joined in when dessert turned out to be mescaline. Tripping was the ultimate escape. Where it took me, the sorrows of society could never follow.

I found myself surrounded by stars, as I had been in my very first trip. Only this time I was perched on an incredibly high pinnacle, a needle point of rock so high that the earth seemed a tiny green pea zillions of miles beneath me. At first I clung to the rock for dear life, looking yearningly at the stars, which seemed unreachable. And then, my attention caught by the brilliance of one special star, I forgot myself and stood on tiptoe to reach toward it. It was all that mattered, all I could think of. So anxious was I to reach it that I forgot to fall downward or to grab for support and instead I spread my wings and flew. My wings? I had never known I had wings before. They were immense butterfly wings, sprouting from my shoulder blades, colored every color of the rainbow, like stained-glass church windows, but as strong as steel.

I didn't have time to examine them. I was too pre-occupied with concentrating on the star I had to reach. I simply flew. The tiny pinpoint of light grew larger and brighter as I approached. It was awesomely distant, and it took all of my willpower to keep moving toward it, trusting in it as I left behind every definition of security and reality I had known on earth. Finally I reached it and found, instead of a ball of burning gases, what appeared to be a pinhole in a black curtain of night, exuding a penetrating needle of light. I had to see what lay behind the curtain. Putting my eye to the hole, I saw . . . absolutely nothing! It was a pure light, undifferentiated into any forms, a benevolently beaming white radiance that filled me with awe and with a kind of certain love I had never known myself capable of before. Deep inside me, I wept with joy. I didn't "crash" after that trip. I awoke suddenly and floated gently toward dawn.

In the morning we discovered that while we had all been occupied, all of GAA had been looking for us. There had been a riot in the gay section of The Tombs, Manhattan's men's prison, and no one knew what to do about it. The officers agreed never to trip en masse again.

9

I WAS TRIPPING ON ACID IN A STRANGE MAN'S BED when they came to tell me my mother was dead.

I had met him at "the trucks," parking lots near the waterfront whose dark recesses were turned into an urban meat rack, which was convenient if not comfortable for stand-up orgies, and this was only our third date. Our bodies liked each other, and we balled for hours on end.

At three o'clock in the morning his doorbell rang. It was my erstwhile lover Bud and my housemate Joe Murray.

"Sorry to interrupt," apologized Joe.

"Your brother called The Firehouse hoping you were at the dance," Bud explained. "He wants you to call him at this number."

"Now?" I asked, not even bothering to question how they had tracked me down.

"It's an emergency," Joe said.

I dialed the number, not knowing what to expect, my mind racing into terror with psychedelic swiftness.

"Ira, it's Arnold. What's the matter?"

189

"We lost Mother yesterday."

"What do you mean?" I asked, completely bewildered.

He started to cry.

"Tell me what happened," I pleaded, frightened.

"I've been trying to reach you everywhere since last night. Mother is gone. She had a heart attack at the beauty parlor, and they couldn't save her. She died just after they got her to the hospital."

Absurd, I thought to myself. My mother is only forty-seven years old. How perfect, to die in a beauty parlor. My mother is dead. My mother the spider. My mother the goddess. My mother the greenhorn. I have no mother.

I began to cry. They took the phone from me. Bud held me in comfort. Joe found out the details of the funeral. My date stood aside, concerned, but not close enough to deal with the chaos that already reached to the core of my history to open the eternal, unanswerable questions released by the wrenching suddenness of death: *Who am I? Why is this happening to me? Where is my mother?* My trip came crashing down around me. I had to be sober. I wanted to be oblivious. I needed to sort out the real from the horrendous; only the horrendous was the real, as if I had stepped through the silver screen and found myself in a horror film with no way to shut off the projector.

After much confusion and more calming, I reached a plateau of tolerable bewilderment that would allow me to function. I began at any begginning. It was Sunday, November 14, 1971. The funeral, according to Jewish custom, was that day. There was no time to collect myself. I had to get to Lakewood, New Jersey, and I would have to face it still tripping. I smoked as much marijuana as my lungs could hold and kept myself as stoned as possible for the duration.

The rest was a rush of phone calls and hurrying home to the packing and sudden fits of tears. Vito drove me to my uncle's house in Lakewood, along with Bud, Joe, and Dave, our housemate. It was the longest ride of my life.

I arrived to find Ira standing outside. We wept in each other's arms, closer than we had ever been. We sat down, and he told me about the last months of her life. She had given up on Frank's hopes for making a living and opened a real estate office, once again starting out on her own as she had in the dry-cleaning shop when she was sixteen. It didn't do very well. But through it she had met a married man who was interested in her, and only weeks earlier she had flown to Miami for a tryst that, like most of her dreams, had turned to ashes. She came home to Frank. The morning of the day before she died, she woke up and announced to him, "You know what? This is my lot in life, and I accept it. I'll probably never be rich, and I'll probably never fulfill all my dreams, but I want to stay with you. And we did have a good time while it lasted, didn't we?" She had given up her lifelong struggle for perfection, for security and status and Hollywood romance. She had decided to settle for plain old reality, and it had killed her.

The funeral parlor was filled with relatives I hadn't seen in years. I didn't know my mother's brothers and sisters nearly as well as I knew my father's. We had trouble recognizing each other. I had to explain who I was. Frank was there, speaking of her in a sanctified hush. And my father was there. I rarely saw him anymore, since he had moved to a hermit's life in East Orange. He was unwilling to speak to Frank, insulted at being shunted aside at the funeral of his only wife. But I could offer no more than a word of comfort to him and to Frank. Ira needed the most attention. He was bereft. And I needed some myself. It wasn't easy to look in that coffin, but I had to. I had promised. My mother had had a fear of being stricken with some rare disease that made her appear dead, a fear of being buried alive. At her own mother's funeral she had made me open the casket to check for signs of breath, and she had made me promise to do the same for her.

She was all in white, her bleached hair pulled neatly back. An expression of bitter sternness had not been erased by the cosmetician's artifice. Her chin was thrust forward as if in anger, beneath a mouth drawn into a hard, thin line. Her face probably showed the signs of struggling with the immense pain of a massive heart attack, but I fancied that it showed instead an anger at the fate that had robbed her of her dreams, an unwillingness to finish living without trying at least one more time, a defiance in the face of death itself. I looked at her for a very long time. Was this the formidable opponent who had shaped my life with such force? She seemed so tiny in her coffin, so helpless in her final fury. I leaned close and listened. There was no hint of life. My mother was dead.

As I watched her coffin being lowered into its narrow grave, I wept for what was unresolved between us. There would be no final chance to win her approval and respect, to convince her that I was a happy, healthy human being, and not the sick failure she had assumed. Although I had won the right to my own life, this part of the battle had never been conceded. She was going to her grave in the false belief that she had fostered a child of shame. I have not yet been back to the cemetery for a visit.

The next few days were surrealistic. Twice a day I said Kaddish, the prayer for the dead, though its words held no meaning for me, as an atheist. I was praying to someone else's idea of God, surrounded by a few old Jewish men who were glad to count Ira and me among their *minyan,* the ten men required for a congregation, whom they had a daily difficulty assembling in a world that was changing too rapidly for them. I couldn't wait to leave. Jim came down on a bus to see me home halfway through the week of mourning, and I finished sitting *shiva* not according to tradition, but in my own way, playing sad Yiddish melodies on the piano back at Spring Street. I ignored the strictures of the synagogue against music as I ignored its strictures against homosexuality.

By the time I was myself again the year was ending, and with it my term of office as vice-president. I had no desire to run in the next election, but Jim did, afraid the organization would fall into disrepair without his firm leadership. His very firmness was what his opponents used to campaign against him. GAA elected as its second president Rich Wandel, a studiously quiet former seminarian, and true to Jim's predictions the fervor with which we had fought for our rights, the solidarity that had cemented us, began to melt almost from the very beginning.

Four days into the new year, four days after my liberation from the burdens of liberation, I fell in love.

It was chilly when Jim and I scurried across Sheridan Square that January afternoon with nowhere special to go. On the Christopher Street side of the park, someone said hello to Jim, and we stopped. He was lanky and smoothly handsome, his features set off by a moustache and framed by his Adam's-apple-length light brown hair. In some strange way he didn't seem quite comfortable in his own skin, but the light that shone in his blue eyes made him beautiful. His motions had an ungainly sort of grace like a giraffe's, hesitant and angular and gentle. He wore boots and dungarees and a dingy plaid woolen jacket that looked too thin because it made him hunch his shoulders against the cold, and with his hands in his pockets, he seemed to be saying, "Who knows?" with a perpetual shrug of resignation, like the rabbis of Warsaw acknowledging the reasons for World War II. And his eyes . . . that special light. . . .

All this while he had been talking with Jim, and I hadn't heard a word. I listened for a minute and joined in with whatever brightness I could think of, but I left my eyes where they were. He heard what they were saying. When the conversation was over, he wrote something down on a piece of paper and gave it to me. It said, "Phil Villani, 434 West St., Apt. 3-C."

"I have no phone," he explained, "but whenever I meet people I think I can communicate with, I give them my address. Drop by if you like."

"I will." I smiled.

When he had gone, I asked Jim who he was. "Oh, just some friend of Tom and Marty's," he told me, "but he has problems."

Ignoring the warning implicit in Jim's observation, I went to visit Phil the next afternoon. His apartment was in a tenement building facing the warehouses that squat into the Hudson River. To add to its isolated land's-end feeling, the building stood alone on its block between a parking lot on one side and a closed gas station on the other. The staircase inside sagged with age and announced my arrival with rising squeaks. It was a tiny apartment, one room with an alcove for a kitchen and a view of the West Side Highway. Everything was in disarray. A bed composed of plywood and sponge rubber was the only furniture, and Phil was building a dresser in the middle of the room. His activity reminded me of Grandpa Simon, who had kept his hand in carpentry by refining an occasional piece of furniture while I lived in Newark.

We slipped into conversation as easily as I slipped out of my coat. It was as if I came there at two o'clock every afternoon, and we were simply picking up the thread of the previous day's discussion. I spoke rapidly; he listened steadily, understanding me as thoroughly as anyone I have ever met. We meant the same thing by the same words, the sort of communication that delights me most. We talked for thirteen hours. We told each other our lives.

"I spent seven years studying for the priesthood," he told me. There was a moral integrity about him, a firm but gentle honesty that appealed to me more and more, especially when the conversation grew personal. "I'm just getting over a suicide attempt," he said with simple candor.

"I tried it twice," I answered.

"But that isn't all." He coughed and cleared his throat hesitantly. He did that a lot, as if he were perpetually saying a polite "Ahem" to excuse himself. It made him seem shy. He continued, "I flipped out first, all the way. I mean I even went to the door of the Men's Federal Prison up the street and tried to get in. Ahem. Because of what the tarot cards said. Did you ever have your cards read?" I nodded. The tarot was in fashion. He went on. "I'm a Sagittarius. How about you?"

"Me too," I said, but I was busy thinking how gracefully he went about being a carpenter.

"What do you live on?" I asked.

"I drive a cab. I used to teach third grade, but with my record I don't think they'd trust me again."

"I teach English."

"I have some poems I've written," he offered. He fished them out from where they were stored. They were about a painful love affair with someone named George. "George is an artist," he told me. "He turns everyone on. He was married, and he has a son, but he's separated from his wife now. We were buddies. We hung out together."

"Did you sleep together?"

"Ahem . . . yes."

"Then you weren't buddies; you were lovers."

"I don't like to label things."

"The name isn't important. The facts are. It's something I learned in the gay liberation movement."

"I don't much like the gay world," he said. "I don't act like that."

"The 'gay world' is how all of us act, including you. That's the point of being open, to change the definitions and the stereotypes."

"But I've slept with women too. Maybe I'm a bisexual. Anyway, I haven't slept with anybody for about six months now. I need to get my head together first. That's why I'm making a dresser and baking my own bread. It's sort of like occupational therapy."

I didn't see the therapeutic side of his endeavors so much as the self-sufficiency they represented. I managed not to mind that we didn't ball, even if it was a little frustrating. Finally, at three in the morning, he drove me home in his old panel truck.

A couple of days later he came to find me at The Firehouse. I knocked over three chairs getting to him. We went back to his house, and when the subject of sex came up, he rose and quietly took off all his clothes and stood there as if to say, "This is my body. Disappointing, isn't it?" He thought his cock was too small, his hips too broad. I saw an appealing Botticelli sinuousness in his slouch. But when I reached for him, nothing happened. I decided to chalk it up to his seminary training. Just being with him was satisfying. The sex would come later, I decided. I loaned him some books about gay liberation, as much with sexual as with political motive. We began to date regularly.

When the General Welfare Committee announced that it had decided not to report Intro 475 onto the floor of the City Council for consideration, Phil understood my anger, even if he didn't share it. I had Jim to share it with. He had moved into the top floor of the house on Spring Street with me, and we created our own subsidiary ménage, withdrawing more and more from the rest of the household to confide in each other. At the end of each day we shared our experiences: his search for a new task to replace presiding over GAA and my search for a way into Phil's bed. Though our terms of office had expired, our ardor for the principles of the movement had not, and both of us continued to practice what we preached to other homosexuals: the virtue of coming out of the closet. There were few arenas left for me to come out in. Everyone in the family knew. All my friends knew. Everyone at school knew, except for the students in my classes. So when the opportunity presented itself in Freshman Composition, what else was an honest person supposed to do?

One of the women had submitted a poem for the class's consideration, a greeting-card type of lyric on love and friendship. When I asked the class for first impressions, one of the men volunteered, "It's okay, but I wouldn't write that kind of thing."

"Why not?" I prompted.

"It's just not right for men to write that kind of stuff."

"You mean love poems? You know that some of the world's most tender love poetry was written by men. Shouldn't men express their feelings?"

"Yeah, but it's just not manly. I wouldn't do it is all. Or if I did, I wouldn't tell anybody about it."

"I think you should be proud of whatever you create."

"But people might call me a faggot. You're not queer. You wouldn't want to be called a faggot, would you?"

I caught my breath as if preparing to dive from a tall cliff into a new sea. "As a matter of fact, I *am* what you call a faggot, but you're right. I don't like being called by that name. I'd rather be called a homosexual, thank you."

I felt suddenly naked. I could see them struggling with themselves. Faggots were to be looked down upon. Professors were to be looked up to. After a difficult silence the questions came, questions about propriety and effeminacy and child molestation and everything but what I do in bed. I answered them patiently, glad to dispel their myths with a little education straight from the horse's mouth.

"But why did you feel it necessary to tell us?" someone asked.

"Because it's true," I answered.

The general response was enthusiastic. A few were horrified, some on moral grounds, some on emotional grounds. Most considered me something of a hero for my honesty, but I felt as if I had done no more than any heterosexual teacher who mentions a husband or wife at home.

After class one of the men came up to me. "I really think that was right on," he encouraged me. "Do your own thing. Your kind is okay. It's the other kind that bothers me—you know, the swishes, the obvious ones."

"I'm doing my best to be obvious," I informed him eye to eye. "When we're talking about choice of sex partners, there is no 'other kind.' "

Some months later one of the women in class came up to me. "Remember what you told our class about yourself?"

"Of course. How could I forget?"

"I'm gay too," she said. We talked for a long time. I told her where she could find information about herself and where there were women she could ask about what a lesbian can expect from the world. Because of her I have made it a point to come out in every class I've taught since then. And in every class there's someone contemplating her suicide, or someone with circles under his eyes from leading a double life, or someone politicized into uncontrollable anger. They all need to be heard. Most of their straight peers are ready to accept them, but many are still confused. The older students are more frequently shocked. Some report me to the deans. Some accept change gracefully. Some, like the fireman who was in another composition class, accuse me of being bigoted in reverse.

Firemen hold a special place in the history of gay liberation. They were especially sensitive about our demands for equal employment rights, because they feared that their practice of waiting for alarms in their underwear would raise questions in the public's mind about their virility if they acknowledged the presence of homosexuals among them. When some of their union leaders attended a dinner given by the Inner Circle, a collection of politicians and press representatives, the feud that had begun with Intro 475 was exacerbated. Part of the entertainment was a skit derisive of gay liberation, and one of our members, who as a politician's aide was present as our fifth column at the dinner, came directly to The Firehouse to tell us about it. We were just recuperating from that afternoon's demonstration in Long Island. I was too tired to protest all over again, but a group ran up to the Hilton Hotel, where the Inner Circle dinner was still in progress, to distribute leaflets stating that there was nothing funny about our treatment at the hands of the press and politicians present. Jim went along with the leafleters, and I went home to rest. I had just settled down when the phone rang. "There was trouble at the Hilton," a member told me.

"Jim wants you to come to Roosevelt Hospital right away."

The leafleters had been attacked by the dinner guests. Two who had seized the microphone to announce the purpose of their presence were stomped right on stage in full view of everyone. Others, including Jim, were attacked and beaten in the hallway and shoved down the escalator. According to all reports, the assault had been led by Michael Maye, the president of the Uniformed Firefighters Association.

The emergency room was like the morning after Dunkirk. Jim emerged from its inner recesses looking terrifying, his eyes swollen green and purple, visible through the bandages that loosely covered his stitches. I swallowed my repulsion and got to him with instant cheer.

"Having a little problem?" I smiled.

"Get me out of here," he said through painfully gritted teeth.

We took a cab back to Spring Street to find Vito pacing anxiously in front of the house.

"I came as soon as I heard," he said, approaching Jim with a fiercely frozen smile and deflecting his glance as soon as it was practical without alarming the patient. Vito is squeamish about blood and guts, and Jim's appearance was enough to make even strangers wince.

We got Jim into the kitchen and puttered around to distract his attention. By the light of home and hearth he looked worse. It was dragging the horrors of reality into our gay sanctuary. Vito and I made cold compresses and hot coffee and took turns crying in the corner behind Jim's back. We did our best to keep him away from a mirror, but he had to look. It didn't much matter, because his picture was soon in all the papers anyway. The affair had become a *cause célèbre* bringing

gay civil rights and Intro 475 to the attention of New
York. The price of publicity, we had learned, was
blood. In a year a thousand of us would appear at the
Hilton Hotel to protest the next gathering of the Inner
Circle and the easy acquittal of Michael Maye.

But the week of the original incident, with what felt
like unparalleled boldness, I demanded of a packed
Firehouse that the organization get off its ass and re-
dedicate itself to the passage of Intro 475. Nonetheless,
my interest had already begun to wane. I hadn't missed
a single meeting of GAA in over two years, and I was
exhausted. I began to miss meetings now and then, and
I found that the world didn't crumble. My personal life
was beginning to involve me more than my political life
although I found the two equally frustrating.

Phil and I had continued to see each other through
these months, but our relationship had become one of
good friends in spite of the passion I felt. He kept busy
with pottery lessons at the studio of a woman named
Marilyn Brown, around the corner from his house.
When we spoke of love, he was more likely to reminisce
about his former lover George than to consider my
petition for his affection. But as long as he wasn't sleeping with anyone else, I felt safe, if not satisfied. There
was no way I could hide the strength of my desire from
him. We were too honest with each other for that. Inevitably a strain grew between us, and both of us knew
it.

"You're in love with a false image of me, a fantasy,"
he proclaimed as April began. "Ahem. . . . You think,
because I drive a panel truck and bake my own bread,
that I'm some kind of counter-culture hero. You think
because I've learned to sculpt ceramics that I'm an
artist, but I'm not. All I am is someone who's trying
to survive, and you want me to achieve. I'm trying to
recover from psychosis. I'm not your Mr. Right."

I remember how guilty I had felt about Alice's patience when she had waited for me to recover from my suicide attempts. I felt as if I owed such compassion back to someone else. Besides, I still loved him. I told him so.

"Ahem. . . . I think maybe we shouldn't see each other for a while," he said.

And so I spent the month of April listening over and over again to "Without You," the torch song of the moment, and feeling thoroughly miserable. For a spark of hope I tried to imagine a brighter future. I was all too willing when a gypsy beckoned me into her parlor to tell my fortune, and as skeptical as I was about the amusement-park proliferation of such establishments in Greenwich Village, I was willing to pay someone a few dollars just to hear what I wanted to hear about the future. I listened carefully as she assured me I was about to take a long journey across the sea. I almost laughed out loud. I wanted to hear about the tall, dark, and handsome stranger that was the fortune teller's stock in trade. She had pulled the wrong cliché out of the deck. One of my earliest childhood fears was the thought of being stranded in a strange place, with a foreign language in which I couldn't even communicate. I wasn't about to take off on my own, even if my sabbatical year from school was beginning. No: I would stay put.

My days had grown empty. When my brother called to say he wanted to pay one of his rare visits, I was glad of the evening's company.

"We opened Mother's vault box," he announced.

"That's good." I said without enthusiasm, expecting little and not too interested in stirring up old pain.

"Well . . . you remember that Mother had two insurance policies, one made out to you and one made out to me. . . ."

"Yes?"

"She cashed one of them in. . . . It was yours."

I couldn't escape the idea that cashing in my policy was tantamount to cutting me out of the will that didn't exist, that not only hadn't I convinced my mother of my validity as a person, but quite the opposite, she had seen my self-acceptance as a commitment to perversion, a frustration of her hopes for my giving her a wife to befriend and grandchildren to be proud of. And now she was having the last word . . . from beyond the grave. I said as much to Ira.

"I'm sure she didn't mean it that way," he consoled. "She probably just needed the cash."

"We'll never know," I answered. *"I'll never be sure."* The thought would never leave me.

In that mood I was relieved when Phil called at the end of our month of trial separation.

"Can I come over to see you?" he asked.

"Of course." I still loved him. I still hoped he could accept me and the homosexuality that relating to me implied, no matter what mothers or anyone thought.

"Remember Marilyn, who I study pottery with?" he asked when he arrived.

I nodded. "Sure."

"I've been sleeping with her."

"Oh." It was all I could say. My only consolation was that at least it wasn't another man. I was being rejected as a lifestyle, not as an individual. But the thought didn't do much to stop the pain. Normalcy is formidable competition. The whole world is on its side.

"Maybe now we can be real friends," he continued.

"That might take some time," I said. He nodded.

It was one of those times when life seems to stop for a long breath. Everything I had been working at had come to nothing. I didn't want to sit in a chair and wonder what was wrong. I wanted to forget. An empty year lay ahead. Only my own efforts could fill it. No one could do it for me. No one was around to do it with me. I needed something new, something different, something far away from disappointment. Europe! The Eiffel Tower, the British Museum, Michelangelo's "David," the islands of Greece. There were people I knew in Europe: college friends, GAA friends, Heidi in Vienna. It would be good to see her now that she knew why our attempt at an affair had failed. I wouldn't be so alone. I planned an itinerary, delighting in the maps that would soon be real places for me.

I called my father to tell him I had decided to travel across the Atlantic.

"I never went," he said. At least I would never have to say that. Within weeks, after a tearful farewell from Jim and Vito, I was on my way.

Paris's passing crowd intrigued me. At first I thought all the men were gay. Their manners, their clothes were the standard signs I was used to in New York. But soon I learned they were only being Parisian, defining their masculinity by a completely different guidebook. I had a list of gay haunts in all the places on my itinerary, and when watching other people going about their daily lives grew dull, I tried some of them. I didn't last long cruising the museums and parks. It was like being plunged back into Washington Park in Newark a dozen years before. Then I tried a place called Le Nuage, which was near my hotel on the Left Bank.

Afraid of violating local custom, I ordered *un Pernod* at the bar and simply watched the men who were sprinkled the length of the dimly lit room. In the back there was a small raised dance floor against a mirrored wall, where now and again someone or other would dance alone, watching his image in the mirror doing steps that had long since fallen from fashion in New

York. I imagined some city ordinance against men
dancing with each other and, emboldened by my second Pernod, I rose to dance by myself. I was doing
everything else alone, and at least dancing could provide a familiar feeling to assuage my growing unhappiness. In the middle of the song I found a lithely handsome man facing me, matching my latest step with his
own. At last I had met the real Paris, I thought. After
a few songs we sat down to talk. He lived in Greenwich
Village, a few blocks from my house!

In London the obvious place to solve the problem of
meeting people was at the Gay Liberation Front. I went
to a meeting and a dance, but there were more politics
than pleasure there, and the politics had an all-too-
familiar ring. I was tired of walking around a city full
of people who had each other to talk to and busy lives
to lead. The contrast with my solitude made the loneliness grow until it was almost unbearable. Finally, after
a few days, I took myself in hand. Whose vacation is
this? I asked myself. Just because I planned two weeks
here doesn't mean I can't change my mind. This is my
one chance to do whatever I want, to see whatever I
want. Now what do I really want to see?

I wanted to get away from the city, to be where it
was refreshing to be alone, to see the places that had
inspired the writers I had loved since college. After all,
I wasn't only an American Jewish homosexual, I was
an English teacher too, and I was in England. I went
to a travel bureau and chose three places: Haworth in
the Yorkshire moors, where the Brontë sisters had lived;
Keswick in the Lake District, where Wordsworth and
Coleridge had roamed; and of course Stratford, Shake-
speare's home. My second week in England would be a
literary adventure.

Haworth proved to be a charming town of dark stone
houses set among rolling green fields. The Brontë

parsonage was of passing interest: it was the moors outside town I had really come to see. The landscape was difficult but delightful. Gnarled, scrubby foliage clung desperately to sparse grassland in a wind that never ceased sending an endless row of clouds scudding quickly across the sky. It was a barren place, one where it was somehow healthy to be an individual alone. I walked for hours, feeling cleansed by the incessant wind, strangely refreshed. And in the distance, too far to reach in a single afternoon, I could just make out Wuthering Heights, the house that had inspired Emily Brontë's novel. I listened for the name of Heathcliff, called by Cathy Linton's ghost, but there was only the rushing sound of the wind, and it was enough. I felt a new innocence I hadn't known since I was a child, a gladness that made me hesitate to leave. But there was more to see ahead.

I had arbitrarily chosen Keswick in the Lake Country, knowing nothing about it. At first it was a disappointment, a resort for middle-class families who made me feel self-consciously conspicuous with my long hair and jewelry. I found lodging in a bed-and-breakfast that was run with military efficiency by a stern-faced woman who kept track of her guests with a board of numbers affixed with sliding tags that announced whether one was "In" or "Out." She served meals of precisely measured portions, gliding soundlessly among the tables like a wheeled robot, setting down plates with care, and if someone murmured, "Thank you," she would reply in kind, "Thank you," so that if there were seven polite people in the room, there would be seven thank-yous and seven replies: "Thank you," "Thank you," "Thank you," fourteen times, without another word exchanged.

Derwentwater, Keswick's lake, was beautiful: glass-gray and swept with eerie mists on its surface, encircled by sober mountains puffy with green against the cloudy sky, a wonderful place to walk. It drizzled a great deal, but on a nice afternoon I traveled to the neighboring town of Grasmere, where Wordsworth's cottage was, and I understood anew the "visionary gleam" of childhood that had inspired his poems. The Lake District was the most beautiful landscape I had ever seen, pregnant with a secret spirit that suffused the very earth, lush and promising and peaceful, a fine place to be born.

Yet I was lonely all over again. I felt restrained by the civility that surrounded me. I needed someone to talk to, and I had only myself. I was different, alien. It made me feel uncomfortable, stared at, desperately alone. There was no way to assuage my unhappiness, but there was one way to amuse myself at least internally. I had purposely torn a page of *Europe on Five Dollars a Day* and put several nearly invisible squares of windowpane acid beneath the cellophane tape I had used to mend it. Tripping could turn an afternoon walk into something special, release whatever secret beauties the landscape held.

It was a Sunday morning. My trip began with the accompaniment of a steady drizzle, so I was confined to the guest room to study the flowered upholstery against the flowered carpet, and the pictures of flowers hanging on the flower-printed wallpaper. I tried to watch television: instructions on making toffee, a lecture by a pianist who accompanied lieder singers, and an Episcopal church service. I went out in spite of the rain, stopping for tea at a family restaurant, feeling stranger and stranger, different from everyone around me, American because they were English, Jewish because they were Christian, gay because they were straight. And the way they looked at me, eyebrows slightly raised, made it seem as if they could see it too, as if only their polite restraint kept them from telling me what they thought about my long-haired idiosyncrasies. I wanted to flee, but there was no place to go, no one to go to, no one who knew me and loved me to tell my sorrows to. I was as thoroughly miserable as I have ever been in my life.

As soon as the rain let up, I made my way to the lake, anxious to be alone as I had been on the moors. If there is no one to talk to, then let there be no one to see, I thought to myself. Why am I left alone? Why am I here, wandering in a world where I'm so different? Why do I feel so utterly despised, as if I were the lowest creature on earth? Aren't I a citizen of the universe too, as good as all the rest? Don't I belong somewhere too?

Not with my ears, but with my soul, I heard a Voice, which answered: *"YOU ARE MY CHILD."* And the sun shone more brightly behind the clouds. I knew that I had been praying. And I knew that I had been answered.

I felt comfort and gladness and peace all at once, and a love that surpassed any passion I had ever imagined, a love in which I could rest totally secure. I felt the need of some symbol, some token of those words that resounded in my brain: "You are my child. You are my child." A feather lay at my feet, and I stooped to pick it up, thinking I would take it as a memento of that moment; but it was covered with insects, darting with life, and I felt myself a brother to that life and replaced it on the ground with sober respect. Silently I thought, "Will You give me a sign?"

Again the Voice spoke: *"I AM WITH YOU."* And I felt a surge of strength inside me, certain that the father, the lover I had always dreamed of, was with me, would always be with me, no matter what happened, for the rest of my life and beyond. Still I looked for some token, something to remind me of this day (as if I could ever forget it). And a sense of fear and awe swept over me, as if the material symbol I was looking for signified some doubt of what I knew unshakably to be true. I turned and stepped square in a pile of cow shit! And I laughed aloud, because I had had my sign.

The afternoon was perfection spent in the wet woods and fields and crags that skirted the lake. The day was charged with a current that passed through everything, making the landscape radiant with light. I no longer saw with the eyes I had seen through that same morning. I had ripped aside a curtain and unveiled the truth. I was no longer lonely. I was no longer an atheist. I was something new.

Amsterdam is a homosexual's delight, but I remember it more as a Jew. I visited the house where Anne Frank and her family had hidden from the Nazis until their capture and their internment in the concentration camps. I had read Anne's diary, but as I climbed the stairs to the secret annex, I knew it was more than a literary pilgrimage I was making, more than a visit to the site of a movie. The pieces of my mind felt a special kinship with Anne Frank. I was a Jew. She had been a Jew. I had been keeping my journal of private thoughts. She had written a book that had moved the entire world. But in her own special corner of the annex, I saw the real link between us: the fading pictures of movie stars she had pasted on the walls. We were both dreamers. I tried to understand the hatred that had killed her, but all I could feel was the haunting sadness of her murdered dreams. I tried to be angry, but only wistfulness would come. I tried to envision the holocaust that had taken millions of lives, but it hurt too much to bear. It hurt all the more because of those faded photographs on a young girl's bedroom wall.

Memories flooded me on the train to Vienna. As I watched Germany's Rhine Valley streaming outside the window, strung with turreted fairy-tale castles, I remembered those photographs on Anne Frank's walls, and the photographs of emaciated bodies falling by the hundreds from wheelbarrows into anonymous graves, their limbs aflail, and the vision of Grandpa Simon presiding over the Passover seder while laughter swept the table from one end to the other, pursued by songs. I didn't want to set foot in Germany. There was too much sorrow waiting there. Vienna would be experience enough. Memories waited there too. I wondered what Heidi would be like after the years that had changed me so much.

She met me at the station. She looked exactly the way she had looked the last time I had seen her. As if only moments had intervened, we were friends again, gossiping merrily. While she was at work, I visited the sights—Beethoven's apartment, Freud's house, the castle at Schönbrunn—but as soon as she was free, she insisted on escorting me everywhere, delighting in my delight as I tasted wines and sampled strudels. But when we went to Vienna's most popular gay dance bar, Die Bruecke, things were different. The ambience was mixed, straight couples blithely mingling with gays; but as tame as it seemed to me, it was too much for Heidi. Within five minutes she fled for the door, taking me with her.

"It's my former boyfriend," she explained in her dulcet Austrian accent when I confronted her about it at home. "He goes zere sometimes wiss his new wife. I was afraid to run into zem."

"I think you left for other reasons," I charged. "I think you were threatened because it was gay."

"*Ja,*" she answered instantly. "I'm sorry. When you wrote how you were, it was fine. I was happy zat you were happy. But I felt funny. I didn't belong."

I was angry. "I feel that way wherever I go. I'm

always different. I never belong. If it isn't being an American in Europe, it's being a Jew, and if it isn't that, there's always being gay." Then I thought to myself, And if that isn't enough, there's always the fact that I hear voices. I'm afraid even to say it. She'll think I'm altogether mad.

"I'm sorry," she whispered. She was weeping. "I didn't mean to hurt you."

"I'll be all right," I assured her. "But I want to belong somewhere too."

One place I didn't belong was the streets of Vienna. I felt an icy hostility greeting my long hair. Heidi felt it too. She explained that Vienna cherished conformity the way Greenwich Village cherished the unique. She was used to being criticized for the shortness of her skirt hems and used to defying the critics, but it was a losing battle, and she knew it.

I spent more time in the house, weary of sight-seeing. All the churches and museums were beginning to run together in my mind, and there were more ahead. I picked a book from Heidi's shelf and began to read. It was a familiar book by Alan Watts, *The Way of Zen*. It reminded me of lessons I had learned before and needed to learn again. It spoke of identity and experience, and I reconsidered all the grief I had been giving myself about who I was. I saw that I had been looking at my own life through the eye of a housefly, divided into a hundred separate compartments like a hundred separate lives. I saw that if I paid attention to what I was doing instead of always asking myself who was doing it, my chances for getting it done would be much better. As soon as I stopped worrying, I began to relax, to put my pieces together again.

I felt so good that my trip though Italy was pure sunshine. I was traveling alone again, but it didn't make the slightest difference. I felt free, happy, glad I had come to Europe, even when I heard an Italian version of "Without You" on someone's radio, and I thought of Phil.

A benevolent moon watched over the Acropolis when I arrived in Athens. There I met Joe Kerstein, my friend from home. Together we visited the Plaka, where a hundred cafés poured their noise into the night. The heat hung still and heavy in the air.

"My hair is hot against my neck," I complained. "And frankly, I'm getting a little tired of being stared at. What's so unusual about long hair anyway?"

"Maybe they're not used to seeing long hair with a balding scalp," he answered honestly. "They're probably used to seeing long hair only on young students."

In the morning we flew to Rhodes. My first stop was at a barbershop. The tresses that had brushed my shoulders like a silken kerchief floated to the floor. I was afraid to look into the mirror, steeling myself, telling myself that I wasn't losing hair but gaining baldness. When I got to the *pensione* where we were staying, I shaved off what was left of the scraggly top, and I looked through my orange glasses to see what I had wrought. I liked it! It was who I was. It was honest, and it looked good because of it. We went off to meet David Sklar, Joe's lover of ten years, who was arriving from a trip to the Middle East, and as glad as I was to see him, I could feel my happiness evaporate as I watched them kiss hello. Suddenly I felt alone again. When we shopped in the local store and they bought matching rings, I felt it even more. Whatever light I had felt at Derwentwater seemed extinguished, but I carried on the best I could.

I was almost glad to leave the capital city for a motor-scooter ride on the open road. We left the flowered lushness of Rhodos behind and chugged into the arid countryside beneath the hot sun, aiming for

Lindos, a town everyone told us we would love. We passed tight-mouthed women, their heads wrapped in scarves that wound around their necks, sitting on slowly moving donkeys. We stopped to eat grapes beneath a tree. I had no experience with motor scooters, but I just relaxed, and things generally took care of themselves while I let my imagination wander, thinking of what handsome olive-skinned farmers had traveled the same road centuries before on roughhewn carts, their muscles glistening in the sun, their strong arms. . . . Suddenly I realized there were two ladies walking in front of me, looking as if they had just stepped out of an English garden. I panicked, forgetting how to stop and dragging my sandalshod feet on the road until they were bloodied, narrowly avoiding the two women. We had arrived in Lindos.

By evening I found that I was also sunburned and that my hands were thoroughly blistered from holding the handlebars so tightly. We spent the next morning sight-seeing, but when it was time to leave and I had to pass the spot where I had almost hit the two women, I froze. Joe and David were well ahead. A bus was coming toward me on the narrow road, and to avoid it I drove too close to a wall, scraping my leg bloody until the bus had passed. I barely made it to a stony patch a few yards beyond, where the scooter spilled me onto the gravel, embedding pieces of it in my blistered hands.

Joe and David came back to find out what had happened to me. We put the scooter together the best we could, but I refused to climb back on it. "If there are buses here, there are buses out of here," I insisted.

"You have to get on," David said. "You have to return the scooter."

He was right. I was being silly. I got back on as gingerly as possible, ignoring the sunburn, favoring the bruised leg, gripping lightly with my sore hands wrapped in wet handkerchiefs. I moved forward as slowly as I could.

When we came to a sign that said in miraculous English, "TO BEACH," David said, "Maybe a little salt-water will be good for your scrapes." I nodded. "TO BEACH," however, does not mean "Fifty Yards to Beach" or "Directly to Beach." We found ourselves on a steep downhill road that wound its unpaved way for what seemed miles of precarious ruts whose stones were flung like shrapnel by our wheels. My motor conked out three times in spite of the downhill incline, but eventually we made it to a tiny beach with a restaurant where we swam and rested and ate, all painstakingly in my case.

When it was time to go, we started uphill. Joe and David had disappeared ahead in the hot dust when my motor stopped again. It was too hot to just stand in the open sun, so I began to push the scooter up the hill, sliding in the ruts, wishing for more than an occasional olive tree to protect me from the white-hot sky, which seemed to drain my energy while it attacked my bruised flesh. The road wound sharply, leaving the past and the future out of sight. There was no sound beside my own breathing in the afternoon haze. I stopped to wipe my brow, slowly realizing that here was a childhood nightmare come true. I was alone, lost in a strange place where I didn't even know the language to ask for help. I was ready to give up, to lie down by the side of the road and die, when suddenly there was a sharp pain in my leg. I had been stung by a bee!

There was nothing left to do but laugh, and I did. Things couldn't get any worse if they tried, so they would simply have to get better. Just then, as if by magic, a farmer's cart appeared behind me, stirring the dust. I flagged him down, determined not to let a little thing like language prevent my rescue. "Kaput," I said, pointing at the scooter and separating my hands in a butterfly stroke to indicate finality. "Kaput" he understood, and with a good deal of grunting and sweating I found myself perched in the back, holding the scooter among the boxes of vegetables he was carrying and trying, in spite of the jouncing, to smile at his wife, who eyed me suspiciously from within the folds of her scarf. That was how Joe saw me when we passed him in the road where he had stopped to wait.

The gas station attendant's method was to turn the scooter upside down and shake it. I had hopes that he wouldn't be able to get it fixed so that I could take a bus, but somehow he managed to get it running. It was already late afternoon by the time he finished. We had a long ride back to Rhodos, and we had to get there by dark, or we wouldn't be able to negotiate the treacherously curved roads since the scooters didn't all have headlights. There was terror in my mouth as I climbed back onto the scooter, but this time I was determined. It was me or the scooter. I had to control it. No! I had to control myself.

I remembered Alan Watts's advice that I had read in Vienna, and I concentrated not on who I was, but on what I was doing. I allowed myself to think only of where I was going, and amazingly, steadily, I made my way to Rhodos, triumphant.

A few days later we flew to Crete, stopping in Heraklion to visit the ruins and then heading to the tiny town of Matalla on the southern coast, through arid valleys where time has broken down like an old truck. Matalla was primitive, and splendid because of it. Young people from all over Europe gathered on its little beach, which was embraced into a cove by a long arm of sandstone cliff into which were carved rows of caves that had once been inhabited. Inside them the stone was fashioned into rooms, complete with stone pillows affixed to stone beds. It was like staring another aeon in the eye. The cove faced west into the sunset, and each night, as the sun sank with peaceful colors into the sea, all the visitors in town lined up along the beach to watch its magic.

It seemed to aim for the horizon just past the sandstone cliff, but every night when it reached there, it revealed in silhouette, for only several precious moments a day, another spit of land wrapped in purple haze. I looked, but I made no effort to reach it. I knew what it was. For me it was Utopia: Shangri-La, Camelot, the *Goldene Medina,* Wonderland, Sherwood Forest, Never-never Land, Oz. It was a place to dream of but not to live in. The journey back home from there would be too strenuous.

Once the sun had set, the electric Mediterranean blue was all darkness, and the young people made a beach fire and sang their songs in many languages around it. On our last day there we celebrated the evening magic with the last of the acid. I looked up to a sky suddenly full of stars, as many as I had ever seen. A line from a childhood song ran through my head: "Someday I'll wish upon a star and wake up where the clouds are far behind me."* From the myriad of twinkling lights, my eye chose one, and the singing and the beach went away.

I saw nothing but that star before me, a pinpoint of light, waiting. I yearned for it with all my mind, straining. Once I had flown in a vision to a star and seen in it the radiance that was perfection. That light had somehow illuminated everything since. I wanted more than anything to see it again. I strained even more. I be-

* Copyright © 1939, renewed 1966 Leo Feist, Inc., New York, N.Y.

came nothing but the will to reach the star, my body cast behind me like a rocket's fuel. It cost me every iota of energy I owned and more, straining to the point where I knew I might lose myself and die, straining to reach the most beautiful white light and touch it once more. Straining until I was all the way there, looking through the curtain of night as I had before, and I wanted to go Home to it, to my Father, even if it meant to die. Using energies I hadn't known were mine, I forced my conscious way into the hole in the night that was the star, through it, down a tight channel, as if I were being born into the radiance, straining until I knew I had pushed all the way through to the other side. I opened my eyes, expecting to see perfection.

I saw the beach at Matalla. I saw reality, and it was beautiful. There was the sound of young people singing. The next day I began the trip home to America.

10

"HOME," AS GLINDA THE GOOD TOLD DOROTHY, "IS where the heart is." The day after I arrived back in New York, I met Phil walking down Christopher Street. We sat on a doorstep and talked for hours, glad to see each other after our separation. We had both changed our appearances. He had grown his hair long while I was having mine cut. He looked more beautiful than ever to me. And within the week I ordered a pair of round rose-colored glasses to replace my orange ones, so that everything looked beautiful, if slightly unreal, all the time. We started dating regularly again, but still there was no sex beyond one fumbling attempt in Phil's kitchen, and soon I was as frustrated as ever.

My interest in sex diminished anyway when I discovered that among the souvenirs I had brought home with me was a sterling case of dysentery which kept me close to the house on Spring Street for most of the next six weeks. It wasn't too pleasant a place to be. Larry, the youngest member of the household, had taken a lover who was given to staging dramatic domestic quarrels, replete with screaming and fistfights in the hallways at three in the morning. Eventually the two of them left, but by the time they were gone, everyone in the house had been drawn into the quarrels over who should replace them and what room belonged to which tenant. Jim and I kept to ourselves upstairs, planning a trip across America. He was tired of New York, and I was half-heartedly hoping to find another Oz, perhaps a rural gay commune where beautiful rugged men tilled the fields with the same strong arms they used to embrace each other, someplace where I could live and never return to the disappointments of New York.

The Third Annual Christopher Street Liberation Day parade had taken place without me, while I was away, and so had the second refusal of the General Welfare Committee to report Intro 475 to the floor of the City Council. Gay Liberation was a long way off. Jim and I set our departure date for the beginning of October. We would travel by train to the West Coast, stopping wherever we chose.

I made the rounds of old friends to say good-bye: Gerry, whose best man I had been; Herb, who had saved my life; Teresa, to whom I had first come out of the closet; Alice, who had loved me. But saying good-bye to Phil was the most difficult. There was something strange about him. It was just a few days before I was about to leave, and we were at his apartment getting ready to go out for dinner before going up to visit Vito.

"How can you meet people on a train?" he wanted to know.

"We'll be staying with gay liberation groups almost everywhere we go. We have contacts all across the country," I answered.

"Christ, don't you ever think of anything but gay liberation?" he said. "You always make such a big deal about being a fag."

I saw red. "I don't care what you think about yourself, but if you have any respect for me, you won't use that word. . . . I take that back: I do care what you think about yourself."

He rose and with a sweeping flourish that encompassed his apartment asked, "How do you like my theater-church?" He had redecorated in intense colors that seemed to thicken the air like veils, vivid blues and purples in the main room, clashing with an orange-and-brown kitchen. The furniture was found objects: wooden crates, concrete blocks, and tin cans arranged into functional forms.

"Very nice," I offered as faint praise.

With reverent and graceful ritual he proffered a button on a tray made of a paint-can lid. "Eat of this; this is my flesh," he intoned. I shrank back, unnerved by his strange intensity. "Afraid?" he asked. There was a cruel glint in his eye. He changed into a different pair of dungarees, put on an old cowboy hat, and faced me, toying with a leather belt. It was as close as he had come to anything sexual, but its sadistic overtone was more taunting than seductive.

"Let's go out to dinner," I said, "or we'll be late for Vito's."

In the middle of dinner he announced suddenly, "I've been seeing George again." I was silent. "Ahem . . . don't you want to know why?" he urged, a hard edge in his voice.

"Why?"

"Our relationship is perfect," he said proudly. "We are complete mates. We belong to each other: it's in our cards. Listen, I promised to drop by his place after dinner. Do you mind coming along?"

I boiled over. "I damn well do mind. I don't want to see him."

"Would you mind waiting outside then?"

"Not for one minute," I said. "Maybe we're not going to make it, but I know George is no good for you. He's treated you like shit. Besides, if you had any respect for my feelings at all, you could never ask me such a thing. It's insulting."

We went to Vito's house, but instead of acting like polite company, we made Vito into the audience of our farewell. We yelled accusations at each other until three o'clock in the morning, unearthing grievance after grievance. It was our way of saying good-bye.

He came to my house early the next day.

"I meant what I said last night," I told him. "I can't go on this trip unless I'm free of you. You don't want to have me, and you don't want to let me go. You can't have it both ways."

He left, but he was back in a few hours, heavy-lidded with barbiturates. He fell asleep on my floor. I covered him. In the evening I woke him and fed him some supper. Then I saw him to the door.

"Ahem . . . I'll see you again before you leave," he said.

"No," I answered firmly. "I meant what I said. I love you. But I don't think we should see each other again."

"If that's the way you want it," he snarled, turning from the doorstep on his heel.

Vito threw a surprise party for Jim and me the night before we left. He spent the better part of it crying in the bathroom. Both of his best friends were leaving. He must have felt like a triangle with one corner. He promised to meet us at the train station to say good-bye, but we knew he was lying, and he knew that we knew.

I was all packed before noon. Our train left at four. As I sat trying not to think of what I was leaving behind me, the phone rang. It was Phil. "I'm at St. Vincent's Hospital," he said, ". . . in the psycho ward."

"I'll be right there," I told him.

Jim came with me. The nurse led us to where he sat listless in his room. He had chopped off his long hair unevenly as if in an attempt to maim himself. His moustache was gone. The story was confused. There had been a fire in his apartment. He was turning the room into a kiln, he explained, to bake his clay pots. Summoned by angry neighbors, the police had broken in through his window.

"But I'm all right," he told me. "My mother was here to visit. Ahem . . . I'll probably be out of here in a few days. Ahem . . . do you want to see what I made?" Shuffling in his paper slippers, he took us to the corner of the recreation room, where he had assembled a shrine of trash and knickknacks, and a painting that ran off the edges of the paper onto the wall. "You look good," he said to me.

"You know I still love you," I told him. I had nothing else to offer. He nodded, but the light in his eyes was dim.

"You've got to catch your train," he said. "Ahem . . . will you write to me?"

"Of course."

I made it to the elevator before I began to cry in Jim's arms. And I cried in the street, and again when I got home; but there was nothing I could do.

Jim and I toasted our future with champagne the first night on the train. I didn't want to look back.

We visited Jim's family in Chicago. We stayed with Movement leaders in Minneapolis, where Jim met someone pleasant, to whom he wrote as we continued on. We walked around the lakes of Madison, Wisconsin, watching the leaves turn red and gold. We got stuck for two days in Billings, Montana, where the only entertainment we could find was shopping in the five-and-ten-cent store. We stayed with Arthur Wallace, who had once opposed Jim for the presidency of GAA. He was living with his new lover in Seattle, and we all went camping in the pine forests on the shores of the Pacific. All the time I thought of Phil, periodically calling Vito and writing other friends, anxious for news, but there was none. We went up to Vancouver, British Columbia, and down to Portland, Oregon, and discussed gay politics. In San Francisco, surrounded by long-haired freaks, I decided to shave my whole head, asserting my baldness as once I had asserted my homosexuality. In Los Angeles we visited the thriving Gay Community Services Center and the Metropolitan Community Church, where we watched gay couples rising hand in hand to take communion. We went to Denver and Boulder, Colorado, and met new people, but by then two months had elapsed, and we were too tired to go on. We had planned to see the Grand Canyon, but after so much wandering, I only wanted to see someplace I could call home. I had found no Oz, no gay commune that was any better a home than the one I left in New York. I even tried answering an ad in a gay newspaper that began, "Let's pioneer in Colorado." I still hoped for Mr. Right. On the phone he sounded more like Elmer Fudd than like the Marlboro Man of my fantasies. I called Vito. "I'll take Manhattan," I told him.

"Phil's been here asking about you," he said. "He's been in and out of the hospital a few times, and now he just wanders around Christopher Street, dirty and asking for handouts. It scares me to look at him." It didn't matter. I was going home. Home to New York.

As Dorothy learned, "If you can't find your heart's desire in your own backyard, perhaps you never really lost it at all."

Jim went to Minneapolis to try to make a go of it with the guy he had met there. Within a few weeks he was home too.

Five minutes after I arrived at my first stop, Vito's

house, Phil arrived. He looked like a scarecrow dressed in an old suit jacket several sizes too large without a shirt under it in spite of the December cold. Around his neck was a pendant made from a rusty mechanical gear he had found in the street. A Jewish skullcap covered his hair, which was shorn to an eighth of an inch, Buchenwald style.

"Hello, Phil," I said quietly.

"I am the Bishop Kourias," he introduced himself with a flourish.

"Hello, Phil," I insisted. Bishop Kourias, I was sure, was not the sort of person I could love. I bought Phil some lunch.

During the next couple of weeks, we saw each other perhaps half a dozen times. I moved back to the house on Spring Street and began to get acquainted with my new housemate, Bruce Voeller, who had just been elected the new president of GAA, while Jim moved in with another friend. Bruce was a former biology professor who had become a full-time gay liberationist, spurred in part by an ugly divorce suit in which his wife was trying to prevent even weekend visits from his three children on the grounds that we were an immoral household. Since he needed the top floor for their visits, I set about fixing up the former living room as a place where I could sleep and write and have company.

I let Phil come to Spring Street because I was becoming loath to be in public with him, never certain what he would say or do. He knew exactly what would embarrass or offend me, and he seemed intent on doing just that, attacking blacks and women in loud tones and, if that failed, assailing Jews and gay liberationists. With an almost arrogant paranoia he imagined eternal friendships where there was only a charitable bowl of soup and extravagant plots against him where there was only a stranger. My housemates weren't too glad of his company. I tried meeting him at his place. The "theater-church" was in ruins.

The windows were broken, the locks smashed. Even the colors on the walls seemed to have faded. The sink looked like a primeval swamp. The toilet had stopped working long before and was filled to the brim with reeking shit. The only furniture was a ripped, dirty mattress on the floor and an overturned box which he sat at to eat gifts of food from neighbors and to smoke old tea bags, pretending they were marijuana.

"How can you live like this?" I asked, concerned.

"Don't be such a Jewish mother," he said.

"But that toilet. . . ."

"The landlord belongs to the FBI," he explained. "He works with the lady downstairs. I thought she was the best, but she robbed me. Ahem . . . she hates me because she's a nigger."

"I thought she was your friend, Phil."

"Kourias," he corrected.

"What about you rent, Phil?"

"The landlord is a kike. He belongs to the Mafia."

"Listen Phil, I'm getting tired of this. Do you really need to run down blacks and Jews just so you can feel superior? Do you need to attack everyone who loves you?"

"I don't want to be a faggot like you," he flared.

"Be what you want," I said.

"But I'll never love you the way I love George," he said triumphantly.

"No matter how hard you try, you're not going to convince me that your fantasies are true. If George loves you so much, then where is he now? Maybe you need to feel important enough to be chased by the FBI and the Mafia, but the fact is that nobody's after you. You were always telling *me* not to fantasize about you, not to make you into my hippy hero. Now are *you* going to live on fantasies?"

"Who are you to tell me how to deal with my pain?" he shouted in one of those moments of utter clarity granted to the mad. "I know they're fantasies. Maybe I need them. Fuck you!"

"That too," I said, and I walked out.

Two months later I met him on Christopher Street. "I'm going to San Francisco," he announced.

"Have a good trip," I said coldly.

I was busy writing, and the household on Spring Street gave me company enough. There was plenty of human interest at home. Somehow our lifestyle seemed important enough to interest others. NBC sent a camera crew to tape us at dinner—probably the most rehearsed meal we ever ate. To me it was just where I lived. My life, gay commune and all, came from who I was, and if I wasn't doing the Middle-American way, I still was part of America, as much as the friends I had grown up with, who had married and raised families. But the differences looked sharp when I paid a visit to my childhood friend Gerry on his birthday.

Every birthday party I had been to for the last several years had been distinctly short on blood relations. At Gerry's party I was the only friend. The guests included his wife, his two sons, his sister, his father, his uncle, and his mother-in-law. With my red glasses and my shaved head, my arms adrip with bracelets and rings, I looked like an import from Mars. When Gerry's wife introduced me to her mother, whom I hadn't seen for many years, the old woman looked puzzled. "This isn't Arnie," she exclaimed.

"Sure it is, Mom," her daughter urged. "You remember."

She squinted at me through a veil of memory, obviously confused. "Yes," she finally allowed, "but is your name still Arnie?"

I was relieved to get back to my Spring Street reality where I had some vague idea of who I was. A few evenings later I walked into Ty's, one of Christopher Street's most popular bars of the day. My interest in bars was beginning to wane, but that was what there was to do for entertainment. I literally collided with Phil, who was coming out. He looked different, cleaned up, calmer.

"Hello," he said. The light was back in his eyes. We talked for two hours outside the bar oblivious of the February cold.

"I just got back from San Francisco," he told me.

"What did you find?" I asked him in the fluency of our old common language.

"I thought about George and Marilyn Brown and you," he answered. "I guess George and I really hate each other, and I guess I was expoiting Marilyn because I didn't want to be gay. I want to try to connect my sex life with my emotional and intellectual life, and I think that's with you."

I was quiet for a long while. Then I answered, "Maybe now that you're yourself again, we could see each other for a while and hope that things work out. I don't know."

"If you're willing after all I've put you through," he said with a touch of chagrin.

The first time we had sex, he threw his coat over his head in embarrassment while I sucked his cock, but it got better and better over the next few weeks, until I dared to feel secure, even when he didn't show up for a few days. But after he was gone for a week, I called his mother to find out if she knew where he was.

"Phil tried to commit suicide again," she told me. "He went to some hotel and took an overdose of sleep-

ing pills. They found him just in time. He's in Roosevelt
Hospital." It sounded like an episode out of my own
life, but I had no time to reflect on that. I left for the
hospital as soon as I hung up the phone.

"I didn't think you'd ever want to see me again," he
said as I came in.

"Given the alternatives, I'm glad I still can," I
answered.

I visited him every other day for the next six weeks,
and we became closer than ever before. He had been
afraid of being a burden, afraid his madness would return unannounced at any time, afraid he couldn't
resume his life. I did my best to reassure him, to show
him I was on his side, that he wasn't facing his problems
alone. We planned ways in which he could find work
that wouldn't require him to explain the gaps in his
employment history. Finally he got a job loading trucks,
and he came to Spring Street to live with me.

It wasn't long before each member of the household,
one by one, came to tell me how glad they were that
Phil had joined us. His gentle quality seemed to shine.
Everyone could see the light in his eyes. I beamed when
he arrived home from work to kiss me at the dinner
table. I enjoyed our quiet evenings watching television,
except for his snide remarks about homosexuals that
had become fashionable on late-night talk shows. I had
worked too hard to be a human being to put up with
being the butt of somebody's sick humor, so when
Bruce, as president of GAA, arranged an appearance
on "The Jack Paar Show," I agreed to go on national
television to present our side of things.

It was March of 1973, only weeks before the family's
annual Passover seder. I was proud of what I was about
to do, and I called my father to tell him to alert Uncle
Henry and Aunt Ruth and the others to watch.

The show was nothing spectacular. Bruce and Nathalie Rockhill, a lesbian, and I did what we could to educate Paar, who was still afflicted with the Fifties concept that all sex is a dirty joke, and that gay sex is a little dirtier than the rest. "Shouldn't I be offended when a writer like Jean Genet talks about having sex with a goat?" he asked, evidently trying to be erudite.

"If anyone should be offended, it's the goat!" I said, and the audience was on our side.

After twenty minutes of noncommunication, Paar finally gave up. "The rest of the the time is yours," he said. "Say whatever you want."

As nervous as I was, I seized my chance. I looked into the camera and tried to talk to millions of people I couldn't see as if we were sitting across a table in somebody's kitchen. "I'm proud to be a homosexual," I said. "I love a man, and I'm not ashamed of it. I don't want to lie about it. Some of you are sitting next to your own children or brothers or sisters who are gay and afraid to tell you, because they're afraid you won't love them anymore. You may be loving their lies. Why not give them a chance to be themselves?" And to the homosexuals I said reassuringly, "The more of us who come out of our closets, the easier it will be for the rest of us. Things will be better sooner than you think."

I was lost in my own rhetoric, forgetting the facts of my own life, ignoring the fact that all America didn't think the way my housemates on Spring Street thought. The next day my favorite cousin called. "The family saw you on television," she said. "They met, and even though I tried to talk them out of it, they agreed it would be better if you didn't come to the seder."

"But why?" I asked, genuinely amazed.

"It was a terrible fight. Everybody was all upset. They said you were shaming the family's good name. Uncle Henry finally said that as far as the family was concerned, you were dead."

I was hurt. "Tell them what I did was honest," I said, "And that I'm going to go right on doing it. *It's my name too.* Good-bye."

I called my father to ask his advice. "Did you see me on television?" I asked.

"Ah . . . no . . . you understand. My condition was such that I had to go to bed early."

What condition? I wondered, but I continued anyway. "I just found out that everybody in the family is all upset about it, and they don't want me to come to the seder."

"They told me there wouldn't be room for Ira's fiancée at the seder either," he replied, ignoring what I had just told him. "If she's not invited, I think I won't go either."

"But *I* wasn't invited," I reiterated, "let alone Phil, my lover."

"Do you think I should take Ira and her out to dinner?" he asked.

I gave up. "Sure, Dad. That's a good idea."

"Oh, and when the weather's better, maybe in the summer, you'll come out to visit."

Sure, I thought, When the monsoon season is over, and the trails to New Jersey are cleared. . . .

That night my housemate Joe, hearing what had happened, brought me a bunch of daffodils to remind me I still had my friends.

On Easter Sunday, Phil and I went to his family's home for dinner as a couple for the first time. His two aunts gave us a pair of Easter eggs with a card, "To Arnie and Phil." They knew who we were, and if their mores forbade discussion of the subject, warmth and hospitality weren't precluded. There was human welcome even if they didn't understand the politics of gay liberation.

Passover night was gloomy for me. It was my turn

to cook for the house, and I had spent the afternoon making the Jewish foods I loved. I served matzos and chicken fat as if I weren't the only Jew in the house, and everyone joined in happily. It wasn't a seder, but it was a family. No one could tell me that blood was thicker than water.

A few days later the phone rang. It was Uncle Henry, and he wanted to come to visit! It was the first time he had ever expressed any interest in coming to see me in all the years I had lived in New York. The morning of his visit I washed the kitchen floor, remembering his penchant for cleanliness. The doorbell rang exactly at noon. How like Uncle Henry to be punctual. As I went to the door, I remembered that he had imposed on the family his Russianized greeting of men kissing each other wholesomely (though not quite as wholesomely as I had grown accustomed to), but I was afraid to kiss him, afraid he would recoil at my homosexual touch. Besides, he had said I was dead, and dead men don't kiss their mourners. I opened the door to find him smaller, paler than I had remembered, a frail old man.

"Hello, Uncle Henry. How are you?" My greeting was clearly reserved. We shook hands, and he initiated an awkward embrace.

I took him on a tour of the house.

"My lover Phil and I sleep here in this bed," I informed him when we arrived at my room.

"Do you want to go to lunch?" he asked.

We went to a local restaurant. He sniffed at the menu, looking for something without meat, especially without ham. I had never thought of it as a *goyische* place, only as a straight restaurant.

Finally we went back to my house.

"Listen," he began, "whatever became of that nice girl, what's her name? Uh, the blonde?"

"Alice? Oh, she's married now. We're still friends. We see each other for lunch every once in a while."

"Oh . . . ah, now . . . about your . . . ah . . . difficulty."

"What difficulty, Uncle Henry?" I knew we were getting to the point.

"Well, I read of a young man who had an operation, and now they say he's very happy, or rather *she's* very happy as a woman."

"You mean you think I should have a sex change? What for?"

"Er . . . ah . . . this, uh, deformity of yours." He saw my brow knitting into anger. "Uh . . . maybe you don't call it that. You have to understand: I was raised to see things a different way."

"So was I," I said. "But I've changed. I like being just what I am: a gay man."

"Well, maybe some hormone shots?" he tried limply. I knew he was trying to be helpful.

"Uncle Henry, what needs changing is your lack of information. I'm not a thalidomide baby, you know, only a homosexual."

"I'm just not used to talking about this. You have to understand." And then leaning toward me, he whispered, "Listen, tell me: what can two women do with each other in bed? I always wondered."

"I've never been two women in bed, Uncle Henry. You'll have to ask them."

He changed the subject. "How come you wear those red glasses? Isn't it bad for your eyes? And what did you do to your hair?"

I changed the subject right back. "About the seder," I began.

"Oh, yes . . . well, er, let me explain. I feel just terrible about the whole thing. It just wasn't the way it used to be. Your Aunt Joyce said it was going to be crowded, eighteen people, but there were only twelve. You know her son wants to be in a rock band. Well he has some very rich friends, a married couple, and they came to the seder. They came instead of you and your father and brother. I think they're going to give him some kind of financial backing."

He looked ashamed.

I began to understand. "You mean they didn't want any gay freaks at the table to ruin the deal? They wanted to make a good impression, and if I refuse to remain silent, I don't make a good impression?"

"Well, I guess it was important to them. They wanted me to play the fiddle to entertain them, but I couldn't. You didn't really miss much."

"If that's all it was, why did you declare me dead?"

"You know how it is. Everybody got me all excited. I never even saw the show."

"But why Passover? Why do business on a family holiday? I never wanted to split the family apart. I only wanted to do some good for myself and a lot of people like me who are unhappy." I looked up, hearing an unaccustomed sound. Uncle Henry was crying! I gave him a tissue.

"What a fool I've been," he said. "The family has to stay together no matter what. Next year will be different. Next year I'll make the seder. We'll invite Ira and his fiancée and. . . ."

"And maybe my lover, Phil," I tried again.

"And we'll have all the traditional foods. Aunt Ruth can make chicken soup just like Grandma Sarah's. Remember how delicious it was, and. . . ."

I flashed a glance in the mirror to check whether I were indeed invisible, trying to remember I was not alone, that the struggle to be real was shared by others.

A week later I stood in the rain for almost five hours, along with the men and women of gay liberation, waiting for the results of the General Welfare Committee's third vote on Intro 475. I stood on the very spot on which I had been arrested over the same bill two years earlier. We joked about waiting for a puff of smoke to announce a new pope. We waited for glimmers of news. An amendment to exclude teachers. Failed. An amendmend to exempt two-family dwellings. And finally a hand in the window, thumb down. We had been defeated again.

They ran into the street, my sisters and brothers. They leaped in front of moving cars and halted traffic, Rosa leading the way, her mascara running in the rain. And the cops appeared, and the inevitable bust, dragging kicking and screaming gays into the paddy wagons. Our men, clasping each other, screaming, "What right do they have? What right?" Weeping in the streets. Our women embracing, consoling each other.

Dave, at the door, burst into tears of rage when I arrived home to tell him. Joe in a fury declared, "Tonight I call all my brothers and sisters to tell them I'm gay, and if one more anti-gay comment is passed, they won't see me again." Phil came home tired from work to find us waiting for the rest of the household to get out of jail and helping Joe to rip off a mask, a process we knew well. We exulted with him when one brother accepted the news gracefully, "I am a homosexual." We held him close when another brother was glad the bill had failed, glad society would not legalize any further "illnesses." We soothed his rage, our rage. We were his family.

But even our sort of family doesn't stay together always. That year we began to come apart. It began with Phil. Two months after he had moved in, I awoke to find him weeping next to me in bed.

"What's the matter?" I asked.

His face was contorted. He hid it beneath the covers. "I feel so ugly," he said.

"I think you're beautiful."

"You don't see the truth. I hate loading trucks. I'm stuck at a lousy job. I'll always be a marginal person."

"That's not true," I consoled.

"I can't overcome my past. It could happen again at any time. It's eating my mind away. I can feel it. I don't want to be a burden to you. I don't want to hold you back."

"You don't hold me back," I assured him. "I need you."

A few days later I arrived home to find him gone. There was a note. It ended, "I wish I could sign this 'Love, Phil,' but I can't even do that."

Soon after, Dave announced he was leaving the house because it was too overwhelming for him. The rest of us felt betrayed, but we understood what he meant. We had been losing touch with the real world, enveloped in our own gay environment where the disappointments were magnified because the expectations were too high.

I didn't feel very celebratory at 1973's annual liberation march. And it didn't help when everybody started fighting with each other. I was onstage, watching Vito emcee the entertainment and helping to introduce performers. The mood was up, with thousands of people in Washington Square Park to see the show. Behind me I heard a scuffle, and soon Rosa had kicked and scratched her way to the stage, her purple jumpsuit tattered at the edges, wanting to know why she hadn't been first in the parade. But when she finally reached the microphone, her complaints came out as a tame plea for us to remember the homosexuals in prison who needed our help. The women had remained silent, but when the entertainment included a pair of female impersonators, they demanded to be heard as Rosa had, and the leader of Lesbian Feminist Liberation—a group of women who had split off from GAA—denounced all men who derided the garments and manners that had oppressed women for so long. Not to be outdone, the leader of Queens' Liberation, a transvestites' group, stalked to the stage and flung his crown into the audience, bidding farewell to gay liberation as he did periodically. The melodrama was growing tiresome to me. If we couldn't keep ourselves together, how could we join the rest of the world?

How? As individuals. One by one. Each in his own life. Each in her own way. Hopefully with each other's support, but standing on our own independent feet.

That summer, when the lease was up on the Spring Street house, we decided to go our separate ways. It had been a rich experience, but it was done. I felt that I had left Oz, but I wasn't sure where Kansas was. I was still looking for home. When Joe asked if I wanted to share an apartment, I agreed gladly.

We found a roomy apartment on, of all streets, Christopher, only a block from the Bleecker Street apartment I had left two years before. Within weeks I knew I had made a mistake. Christopher Street is no place like home. Too much of a good thing can get to you. I didn't much like stepping into a fantasy world every time I went to the store. It was like falling down a rabbit hole and landing in the baths. I had explored my sexual fantasies enough, and I was ready to return to the life I had once led, but as a new person.

My red glasses had disappointed me, raising my hopes over the rainbow, so I traded them in for blue ones and then for gray, to make the world look even worse than it was, to avoid fooling myself anymore. The Technicolor gay world is beginning to fall victim to its own honesty. More and more tourists are coming to Christopher Street to look, and it isn't as totally gay as once it was, or as glittering. Times change. America is growing up through the resignation of a President and the shaking of its dreams. And I am growing with it.

But I still keep doing my bit. At school I organized a gay liberation club. It lasted a couple of years, but only with constant effort. The students were afraid to be seen with each other, afraid to sit in the gay lounge we had won unless the door was securely closed. I taught a course called "Homosexuals and Literature." Only half a dozen people showed up for it, but I taught it anyway. I no longer expected the Emerald City.

That didn't make it much less painful when the City Council rejected the new fair employment bill, Intro 2, or when The Firehouse burned, leaving only ashes where once there had been a home for gay liberation, full of promise. But eventually, I hope, New York will change. Cities around the country are beginning to pass civil rights bills for homosexuals. States are repealing the laws against sodomy. New York won't wait forever to be fair to all of its citizens.

I still see my gay friends, but I see much more of my straight friends than I used to. Good people are too hard to find to let a little thing like labels interfere. Nonetheless, when Ira asked me to be the best man at his wedding, I greeted the request with mixed emotions. I drove there with my father. I hadn't seen him since my mother's funeral. Now I keep in touch with phone calls and Father's Day cards, holding up my end. Where love is offered, love exists.

Ira was glad to see me. For the first time in years we sat down to talk alone together, an hour before his wedding.

"I want you to know you'll always be welcome at my house," he said. "Anytime you want to visit and stay over, feel free. And bring your friends if you like."

He was a little afraid I would turn my wedding toast into a gay liberation speech, but I didn't. It was his day. Maybe it took getting married to make him feel safe with my homosexuality. That didn't matter: we had made a beginning. Uncle Henry didn't call back the next year. I have Passover dinner at Ira's house now.

But I celebrate occasions like birthdays with my friends. At my last birthday party I looked around, amazed at the mixture of people. The party was a surprise, thrown by Gary, a new friend. Gary is straight, but that didn't stop him from dancing with me. Jim Owles was there, and Vito with his lover, Bruce. Marty Robinson was there with his new lover, who had been a student in my gay literature course. A pair of lesbian lovers who both work with me at school were there. Herb came, and so did Teresa and Aoki, and of course my roommate, Joe.

When we had finished with the presents and the cake, we went up to Vito's to watch a movie. It turned out to be *The Boys in the Band,* the story of a different sort of homosexual birthday party, whose guest of honor, Harold, enters late, announcing nasally to his host, "What I am, Michael, is a thirty-two-year-old, ugly, pockmarked Jew fairy, and if it takes me a little more time to pull myself together and if I have to smoke a little grass before I get up enough nerve to face the world, it's nobody's Goddamned business but my own." I'm glad I'm not like Harold. I might have been, except for a little honesty. These days I face the world without the heavy psychedelics too. I think they've already taught me their lesson. At the heart of fantasy lies the truth.

I grew back my hair and removed my rings and bracelets a while ago, and I returned to tweeds as well. The world will have to take me as I am. And I'll have to take it as it is, unadorned. I finally gave up my gray glasses for horn-rimmed clear lenses. I don't need to make things any better or worse than they already are. Even Dorothy landed with her feet on the ground.

Not too long ago, wanting a word from the future, I went to visit a palmist I had heard was special. As I spread my hand, she looked at it and then looked up into my eyes. "Do you know that you're a mystic?" she asked.

I nodded, captivated, feeling as if I were leaving another closet. I had been studying the subject and with relief had decided there would be no Mystics' Liberation Front, just me.

"You had a relationship from when you were twenty-one to when you were twenty-seven, but it didn't work."

"Twenty-two to twenty-eight," I said. "Her name was Alice."

"And another one that lasted about two years. But that was all wrong for you. It wasn't what you thought."

"Phil," I whispered. Aloud, I said, "Will I meet someone else?"

"You have yourself," she told me. "Love affairs come and go." I had learned that already. "Your best years are yet to happen, but you can't waste your time. You have work to do." She went into the details.

My first job is to find my way home. I'm moving from Christopher Street, away from Greenwich Village, uptown. Maybe there I can find my Kansas and settle down with the facts of life, or at least give it an honest try.